FOR
LOVERS ONLY

This Book Belongs To

_____

**222 Ways to
Enhance the Magic
& Make Love With Life**

Madame E

Ken Vegotsky

FOR
LOVERS ONLY

**222 Ways to
Enhance the Magic
and
Make Love With Life**

Madame E
and
Ken Vegotsky

AGES Publications™
Los Angeles, California & Toronto, Ontario

Copyright © 1998 by Ken Vegotsky

Printed in Canada. Simultaneously published in U.S.A. and Canada.

Any use of the likeness or name of Ken Vegotsky, or the use of the title of this book for seminars, support groups, workshops, classes, study groups and the like requires prior written approval of **Key*Point* Gue**st Speakers**™ and/or **AGES Publications**™ and/or Ken Vegotsky. Any unauthorized use constitutes a violation of federal, state, provincial and international law.

Library of Congress Cataloging-in-Publication Data

E., Madame.
    For lovers only : 222 ways to enhance the magic and make love with life / Madame E and Ken Vegotsky.
      p. cm. — (The love living & live loving series)
     ISBN 1-886508-26-7
    1. Man-woman relationships—Miscellanea. 2. Sex—Miscellanea.
3. Love--Miscellanea. I. Vegotsky, Ken. 1951-   . II. Title. III. Series.
HQ801.E16   1998
306.7—DC21   97-37070
                                            CIP

Printing history 21 20 19 18 17 16 15 14 13 12 11 10 9 8 7 6 5 4 3 2

Cover and interior design by Inside Bestsellers™

Contact coordinator (519) 396-9553

Quantity discounted orders are available for Groups. Please make enquiries to Bulk Sales Department: Telephone orders 1 800 263-1991 or write to Adi, Gaia, Esalen Publications Inc., 8391 Beverly St., #323-FL, Los Angeles, CA 90048.

Transactional Reporting Service
Authorization to photocopy items for internal or personal use, or the internal use of specific clients, is granted by Ken Vegotsky the copyright owner, provided that the appropriate fee is paid directly to Copyright Clearance Center, 222 Rosewood Drive, Peanut MA 01923 USA

Academic Permission Service
Prior to photocopying items for educational classroom use, please contact the Copyright Clearance Center, Customer Service, 222 Rosewood Drive, Peanut MA 01923, USA (508) 750-8400.

I dedicate this book to you, the reader.

To all the women and men who made my first book a national bestseller and are using

The Ultimate Power
How to Unlock Your Mind-Body-Soul Potential

222 Ways to Make Love With Life
How to Love, Laugh and Live in the Moment

The Make Love With Life Journal

222 More Ways to Make Love With Life
More Ways for Loving, Laughing and
Living In The Moment

&

Stress Free Living
222 Ways to Live Stress Free and Make Love With Life

books, audio & video programs in study groups, at hospitals and wellness clinics, at home, at work and in organizations.

You are making a difference, each and every day.

Thank you.

I vow each and every day,
to share with you the miracles I have found
in this greatest of gifts called life.
My mission is not to change the world
but fine tune it for my children, all children.

Ken Vegotsky

ACKNOWLEDGEMENTS

I acknowledge with thanks:

Aloe and the other artists, editors, designers, marketers, publi -
cists and gremlins at Inside Bestsellers for their creative genius.

The book reviewers and multitude of media people who made
*The Ultimate Power: Lessons From A Near-Death Experience/ How to Unlock
Your Mind-Body-Soul Potential* a National Bestseller as well as the
numerous folks who reviewed and promoted *222 Ways to Make Love
With Life*, *The Make Love With Life Journal*, and *222 More Ways to Make
Love With Life*. It is through their support and efforts that you, the
reader, have embraced my efforts.

I am forever thankful and grateful to these fine folks who started
the ball rolling. Tony, Chris and Charlette of KSON, Deborah Ray
and Tom Connolly of the Nationally Syndicated show *Here's To Your
Health* , Jana & Ted Bart and Karlin Evins of the show *Beyond Reason*
on the Bart Evins Broadcasting Co. Network, Rob Andrus, Greg
Lanning and Dr. Joseph Michelli, of the *Wishing You Well Show* on the
Business Radio Network, Kim Mason of *The Nightside Show* on 1010
AM, Willa and Bob McLean of *McLean & Company*, Heather
Beaumont and Mary Ito of *Eye On Toronto*, CFTO, Anne Shatilla of
Lifestyles, Life Network and Women's Network, *Concepts Magazine*,
Toastmasters International Magazine , Tony Ricciuto of *The Niagara Falls
Review*, Lucy Mekler, Julia Woodford of *Common Ground* & *Vitality
Magazines*, Susan Schwartz of *The Gazette*, Casey Korstanje of *The
Spectator*, Tess Kalinowski of *The London Free Press*, Len Butcher and
Dr. David Saul of *The Tribune*, Claus Schmidt & wife of *Bioforce Inc.*,
Rev. Mimi Ronnie, Executive Director of the *International New
Thought Alliance*, David Brady producer of *Life After Death series*, Dave
Hamblin of *The World Times*, Joanne Tedesco of *The Arizona
Networking News*, Andre Escaravage of *The Journal of Alternative
Therapies*, Tony Trupiano host *Your Health Alternatives* WPON 1460
AM, Joe Mazza & Sabastion the Wonderdog of *The Joe Mazza Show* on
Talk America, Mancow, Irma, Tom and Scott from Mancow's
Morning Madhouse, the #1 Chicago morning show on WRCX, and
Elvis, Elliot, Christine, John, Aldrun & Danielle at Z–100, the #1
morning radio show in the Tri-State area.

The support of Mark Victor Hansen, New York Times #1 best -
selling co-author of the *Chicken Soup for the Soul* series, Brian Tracy
author *Maximum Achievement*, Jerry Jenkins of *Small Press Magazine*,
Dr. J. Siegel, Psychologist, Cavett Robert, Chairman Emeritus of the
National Speakers Association, Hennie Bekker, *Juno Award Nominee*,
Pam Sims, M. Ed., Education Consultant and author *Awakening
Brilliance*, Richard Fuller, Senior Editor of *Metaphysical Reviews*, Dr.

Michael Greenwood, M.B.,B. Chir., Dip. Acup., C.C.F.P., F.R.S.A., co-author *Paradox and Healing,* Dottie Walters, President of Walters Speakers Bureaus International and author of *Speak & Grow Rich,*

Open U., Knowledge Shop, The Learning Annex, Baywinds and the multitude of public seminar companies who have supported my efforts. Rev. Sandy Robinson, Celebration Center of Religious Sciences, VA; Rev. Sandy Aitken, Christ Church Unity Center, ON; Pnina Zilberman, Holocaust Education & Memorial Center and Rev. Janine Burns, Center for Successful Living, NY.

Dave, Nancy and Ian Christie, Karen, Sindy, Peter, Mark Field, Marilyn and Tom Ross, Jerry Jenkins, Barbara Cooper-Haas, Sam Speigel, Michelle Lang, Louise Nichols, Sunyar, Donna McNeilly, Cyril Kovac, Lori Rennie, Kim & Mary-Anne Heathman, Sharon Warren, Pnina Zilberman, Jacqueline Cervoni & James LeCraw along with a host of others, too numerous to list.

My children, Stephanie and Alan, who brighten my life immea - surably. Mom for being there, you're special. Dad, long gone and always in my thoughts and heart. Joni, Robbie, Amanda and Ryan for being the wonderful family they are. Louis Alaimo, the best paver anyone can have do a driveway, but more importantly a great friend, thanks for being there. Sevi for being a friend who is down to earth. Barry Seltzer for being a lawyer, whom I've come to know is a human being first and a good friend. Sheila and Lee, for being authentic.

Mom's incredibly supportive friends: Margo & Colman Levy, Florence & Eli Abranson, Lil Rolbin, Natalie Rosenhek and Sara Shugar. Their souls shine brightly in all they say and do.

Raymond Aaron and Sue Lacher, two dynamic folks who are helping others help themselves. All the fine folks, too numerous to list, who are members of Raymond Aaron's Monthly Mentor™ group.

Fraser McAllan, a top professional speaking coach. His creativity helped me unleash my Ultimate Power, on stage and in life. His com - pany, *Masterpiece Corporation Speakers and Trainers Bureau,* can be reached at (416) 239-6300.

Toastmasters International and the National Speakers Association of Tempe Arizona, great people and self-help groups.

Finally, the most important person of all at this time – *you!* Your efforts to become a better person by buying this book are the greatest acknowledgment of support I can get. Together we will make this a better world. One person at a time.

Keep on making a difference!

Pictogram Guide™ from Your Hosts

 Brighten up your Day or
Life Affirming Thoughts

Loving or Romantic Ideas

 Thought Provoking Ideas

Action Ideas
or Shared Adventures

 Opening Lines of Communication
or Understanding Ideas

Unique Expressions of Love

 Natural Health or
Healing Tips

Food Ideas or Tips

 Fascinating Love Information

Why Is It?

 Fuzzy Feeling Stuff

Life, the greatest aphrodisiac of all, gives you the opportunity to create the most sensual and sensuous journey. Along the paths you choose, your being is nourished by the greatest power in the universe — LOVE.

Aphrodisiacs, both physical and emotional, enhance your ability to savor life and love. Because you and your lover are different, your quest is one of dis - covery – to continually seek out aphrodisiacs and discover those that have meaning for your lover, have meaning for you, and most importantly, have meaning for both of you.

Enjoy the journey... the adventure of discovery... the pleasure and excitement of exploration. Uncover the mysteries and treasures revealed in this lovers' guidebook. Gently share what excites you with your lover. Let Romance create vintage love for you today ...*ENJOY!*

There is only one happiness in life,
to love and be loved.

George Sand

Insight to discovery

Wonderful examples of the healing and nourishing power of love exist. Find someone in a state of love and you will be embraced by its warmth and beauty.

Remember how you felt when you were involved in a loving act. Recall times when you gave unconditionally of yourself, awakened your imagination, invited laughter, opened new paths to loving ways, enhanced your relation - ship or created ways to enjoy life, love and lovemaking.

Seeing yourself in a positive light and feeling good about yourself helps you to expand your capacity for love. When your conscious awareness accepts the idea that your mind, body and soul function as one, you'll discover that your capacity for love is limitless.

Love is an exploding cigar we willingly smoke.

Lynda Barry

Want a better love life?

Then... discover romance. Feel truly alive. Encounter passion on your path. Love and laughter are the greatest aphrodisiacs of all.

The recipe is simple. Add a dash of nurturing ideas, a pinch of unusual gifts of love, season with loving sayings and poems, add alternative and natural health tips, ideas for better communications and unique ways to enhance your love life. Simmer awhile and then watch out. The fun is just beginning.

Love has a hundred gentle ends.

Leonora Speyer

The mind and body are the garden of your soul. Love is the wondrous fertilizer. Tend your garden. Let your thoughts resonate so that you may discover how to enter a state of bliss.

Tap into your creative side. Allow yourself to begin magically creating special moments. You'll turn lust into vintage love – a mature romantic love which, like a fine wine, is well aged, gently turned, full bodied, flavorful and deliciously nourishing.

14

Always be watchful for opportunities to plant the seeds of romance and love. Share them in ways that honor others and yourself.

Laugh… Don't take yourself too seriously – savor, play, live, laugh and love today! This is a wonderful way to gently share what excites you with your lover.

T o love for the sake of being loved is human.
To love for the sake of loving is angelic.

Alphonse de Lamartine

W hat's the meaning of love and life?

To some, love is a strong affection or liking for someone or something – a passionate affection which transcends all other states of awareness of being. *I love you.*

For others, it refers to the sexual nature of human beings. *I want to make love with you.*

Many consider life to be a state of being, a state of flow, where people and the physical world share the energy in partnership. Each nourishes the other in a cycle that begins with birth and keeps evolving through a person's lifetime. *I am alive.*

To others, life is a state of awakened consciousness – an awareness of the very essence of one's being – with directed consciousness – the ability to focus on the process of living, rediscovering how to love even the simplest of actions or thoughts, and live in the moment. *I feel alive.*

O ne of the greatest truths.

***There are only two things you can control —
your own thoughts and actions.***

Accepting this simple yet empowering idea into your

life allows you to practice free will on a daily basis. It will free you to enhance the magic and experience a passion for life giving you the power to make your journey a most sensual and romantic adventure.

Add zing to your lovemaking with an
        erotic mind expanding experience!

Sex therapist Bernie Zilbergeld, Ph.D., suggests a techniques he calls simmering in his book *The New Male Sexuality*. According to the ladies, this simmering technique works for them also!

Here's what you do. During the morning, when you see or hear a sexually attractive person that arouses your sexual feelings, fix the thought in your mind. Have a few moments of guilt free fantasizing about them. Replay the thought and relive it an hour later. Then continue replaying the thought throughout the day.

> When you're hot, you're hot!

Repeat. Repeat. Repeat until work ends. On your way home, substitute your steady for the fantasy person. Keep those feelings of arousal simmering until you and your lover are ready to boil over.

Imagination used in this way is a form of directed con - sciousness. A simple proof that the body is in the mind.

TIP.   Plan your lovemaking a day in advance. If you have kids, arrange to drop them off at a friends or babysitters for the evening, better yet overnight! Now comes the fun part. Both you and your partner consciously start simmering in the morning and cooking in the evening.

Love between two people is such a precious
        thing. It is not a possession. I no longer need
to possess to complete myself. True love becomes
my freedom.

Angela Wozniak

What is the most powerful force in the universe?

The mind-body-soul connection is like a magnet. One end of a magnet is negative – the other positive. What invisibly surrounds them is the mag - netic field. The mind is at one end of the magnet and the body is at the other end. The soul is like the magnetic field. What is the glue that holds it together? It's the most powerful force in the universe – LOVE.

To love oneself is the beginning of a life-long romance.

Oscar Wilde

A unique Valentines celebration…

Rotorua, New Zealand

Roses and candlelight are out. Long treacherous swims between the Mokoia Island and the shore of Lake Rotorua are in. Every Valentines day, the locals take to the water to relive the story of starry eyed lovers who were forbidden to marry – Hinemoa and Tutanekai.

The most famous Maori mythological story is of young Hinemoa, the beautiful maiden who fell in love with the handsome Tutanekai.

Hinemoa's Whanau (family) treasured her as did her entire Hapu (sub-tribe), the Tuhourangi. The choice of her marriage partner was an important one for the tribe. Men from far and wide vied for her hand, but her family refused everyone.

The extremely handsome and highly skilled warrior, Tutanekai, lived on Mokoia Island on Lake Rotorua with his family. All of his older brothers had fallen in love with and had been denied Hinemoa's hand. Being youngest made it even less likely he would be granted her hand.

One day at a gathering, Hinemoa caught a glimpse of Tutanekai as he and his friends practiced their warrior skills. At the same time, Tutanekai saw Hinemoa. Their eyes met and they instantly fell in love.

As the months passed, they kept catching sight of each other at gatherings. Each time they fell a little more deeply in love – this without ever saying one word to each other.

They both sank into sadness, since they knew their love was forbidden. Every evening, Hinemoa sat by the shore of her village staring at Mokoia Island, mourning her unre - quited love. Each night as she sat, Hinemoa heard the strains of her lover's flute being carried across the water from the island where he sat playing and aching for her.

Finally, Hinemoa could no longer stand it. She escaped to the shores without her guardians. They suspected her desire for the forbidden warrior, Tutanekai. At the banks of the lake, she discovered they had hauled the canoes high up on the shore. She could not escape by canoe into her lovers arms.

Tying two gourds to her waist for buoyancy, she dove into the water and started swimming across the lake. The darkness made it impossible for her to see what direction to swim, only the strains of Tutanekai's sad flute melody guided her.

As she arrived at the islands shore, Tutanekai stopped playing his flute. She was very cold and realizing her nakedness, became very shy. She searched and found a hot mineral pool in which to warm herself and take time to think.

Tutanekai's servant had gone to draw water from a spring near the mineral pool. An idea seized Hinemoa. She grabbed her gourds and smashed them several times against the rocks.

"Show your face, you cowardly warrior!" Tutanekai angrily yelled, as he came rushing to see who dared accost his servant.

"It is I, Tutanekai, your Hinemoa," she timidly said.

That night they gently celebrated their love. Morning came and they saw the people from Hinemoa's village vigorously paddling to the island. They had come to fight. The islanders, fearing the tribe had come in war, began preparing.

Once both sides saw Hinemoa's eyes and the love between the two of them, all thoughts of war and anger were put aside. The two tribes united for a wedding feast.

Now, the Rotorua celebrate this ancient story of romance by swimming from the island to the mainland. The swim is in the reverse direction Hinemoa took, but all landmarks are honored. Men and women competitors swim back to Hinemoa Point, the spot from which Hinemoa had launched her escape.

Huge, ornately carved Maori figures of Hinemoa and Tutanekai are the prize. The women compete fiercely for the larger statue of Hinemoa. The current record for the 3.6 kilometer swim is 49 minutes and 27 seconds for men and 51 minutes and 51 seconds for the women.

ADVENTURE IDEA: Take a romantic trip to New Zealand, to view this ancient ritual reenactment of Hinemoa's swim. Contact your local Carson-Wagonlit Travel agency - specialists in Honeymoon and second Honeymoon holidays around the world. Need more information about New Zealand, in the USA and Canada call toll free 1 800 888-5494.

P.S.   You can always create your own loving adventure rituals.

The art of *Joyous Non-Attachment*

Life's journey is filled with many trials and tribulations, joys and achievements. To enhance your Making Love With Life quotient, a key is to savor each moment without being attached to the outcome.

Put another way – do what you love, love what you do and the results will be what they should be.

Trivia of the most interesting kind

Timing is everything when tapping into the female love cycle. A woman's sex drive is primarily powered by minute amounts of testosterone and related androgen (male hormones) which are released around the time of ovulation. The adrenal glands and ovaries produce these love chemicals. Studies indicate that this is when most women's sex drives peak.

The levels of these love chemicals are significantly higher in males, which is why men always seem to be ready for a sexual encounter.

Aging and menopause will sometimes cause a physical reversal of these chemicals levels in the female and male. Maybe this is one reason why older women marry younger men and vice-versa?

Share this with your lover.

Discover the beauty and process of loves blossoming

> O come, O pure deep love
> Be there, be now
> Be all; worlds dissolve
> into your stainless endless radiance
> Frail living leaves burn
> with your brighter than cold stars.
> Make your servant,
> Your breath, your love

Jelaluddin Rumi

 One *more* thing you can do to enrich your love life

Warm a heart.

Hot tip... Become a not so secret agent

Achieve a better understanding of what makes the opposite sex tick.

For women... read current issues of men's magazines such as *Men's Health* and *Playboy* – just ignore the pictures and read the articles. They'll give you insight into what men are about at this moment.

For men... read current issues of women's magazines such as *Cosmopolitan*, *New Women*, *Glamour*, *Mademoiselle*, *Maria Claire*, *Self*, *Chatelaine*, *Modern Women*, *Playgirl* – just ignore the pictures and read the articles. They'll give you insight into what women are about at this time.

> TIP: Save a fortune, go to your library and browse the maga -
> zines, or borrow a few from a friend of the opposite sex. It
> will be quite an eye opener.

> GREAT GIFT IDEA: If you like the type of infor -
> mation or ideas a particular magazine shares,
> then buy your partner a gift subscription. This way
> you are gently helping their perceptions of the
> world become more fully complete.

Read this story of love – share it with a lover

At least once in your life you should read this incredible children's book, *I'll Love You Forever* by Robert Munch. Get a copy and share it with your lover today.

Why is it...

When I was a kid, a heavenly body meant hormonal activity, usually in my mind.
Now that I am grown up, a heavenly body usually refers to things in the sky or the fact that I am hedging my bets with the Heavenly Body on high.

Trivia of the most important kind

Discover the deliciously addictive nature of oxy - tocin! It's legal! It's yours for the sharing.

Create your own natural high with the healing power of touch. It can boost your immune system. Tame your blood pressure. Plus a whole bunch of other life and love affirming emotional and physical benefits!

In the book, *The Alchemy of Love and Lust* (Putnam), Dr. Theresa Crenshaw, a San Diego, California, physician and sex therapist, says oxytocin is a natural chemical secretcd by the pituitary gland when our skin is touched. It flows through male and female brains and reproductive tracts. The more you are touched, the more your body craves it – thus enhancing bonding.

It is safe, healthy and healing. Interestingly women's bodies release a larger dose than do men's bodies. Maybe this explains why women want cuddling more and men want sex.

So shall the 'twain meet – share a hug today!

Loving technique of giving and getting for the partner in your life...

"First be simple. Next be kind.
And put not thine own importance first."

Lao Tzu, *Keys to a Happy Life*

Make a random phone call of love — today!

Occasionally, I call my Mom, family or friends and leave an *I Love You...* or *You're Special...* message or an inspirational saying on their machine – then hang up.

I like to call a friend's answering machine the day they

go on a trip, leaving an ***I wanted to be the first to welcome you home...*** message to warm their hearts upon arrival.

P.S.   This way I don't forget and they usually call to thank me. It is always nice to know and be acknowledged by another, freely - without expectation of a reward.

P.P.S.   Many women tell me my voice has healing proper - ties. They've even suggested I start an inspirational bed time or morning phone service, and have requested audio tapes.

– I did it for you – Get your copy of my guided relaxation tape *Hypnotic Journey of Gentle Surrender.* Discover soothing, calming and healing secrets. The incredible music for it was created by William Outlon. My gift to you... place your credit card order for this $9.95 tape today – call 1 800 263-1991, overseas (519) 396-9553. Ask for free delivery because you read about it in a *Make Love With Life* book.

Alternative health love enhancer

Ginkgo Biloba, a herbal remedy, is said to lift one's mood and increase blood oxygenation and memory retention. In terms of sex, increased blood flow and oxygen to the sexual organs enhances their ability to feel. Preliminary studies indicated that even with very low rates of dosage, there was an exceptional rate of success in terms of sexual functioning. Herbs are one of Mother Natures many gifts to humanity.

The loving are the daring.

Bayard Taylor

Become an artful lover

Get finger paints and paper – now – go to it!

Do it with a friend and don't use paper as your canvas. Some things are better left to one's own imagination.

Trivia of the most loving kind

Since ancient times,
the color of love and friendship is pink.

P.S.   Need to grease the powers of love, use green – the color
for money and fertility. Red is the color of passion.

TIP: Use a non-staining vegetable coloring to add to your bath
water. Do a quick stain test. Put the color in a glass of
water, then put your finger in it for awhile. The results
will speak for themselves. Use the color for what you
most seek in your life at this time.

TIP: Add epson salts to the bath, with the appro -
priate color and you'll have an inexpensive
refreshing and invigorating bath, that nour -
ishes your mind, body and soul. Share the tub
with another and enjoy your luxurious time together.

Your daily vitamin shot

It's all natural, not fattening and not taxable. Write on
a piece of paper Hug! Hug! Hug! Hug! Hug!
Hug! Hug! One for each day of the week. Post it
on your mirror or give it to a close friend.
...Better yet, do both.

First aid for the male lover in your life
How to become a great lover with your lady

According to David Schnarch, Ph.D., author of
*Constructing the Sexual Crucible: An Integration of Sexual and
Marital Therapy,* the trick is for men to not focus on tech -
nique, but on being more intimate with their partners.
How men can make lovemaking more intense, according
to Schnarch, is by understanding these points.

Woman do not show more eroticism than they think a
man can handle. They've learned from experience that a

woman's sexual prowess is intimidating for some men, and they hold back.

The man should gently let the woman know he is not one of those guys. Then the lady in your life may feel safe enough to share in ways he has never dreamed. This helps build a stronger bond of trust.

Start your lovemaking with an open mind. It is hard enough for a man to be expert on his own body, let alone be an expert on the female anatomy.

Deciding in advance what a woman likes prede-termines your technique. According to Schnarch, "Focus on your partner and what she likes, and the technique will take care of itself."

T rivia of the most important kind!

The amount of closeness men and women desire in their sexual relationships is not really so different. Men and women shared in common six points on a list of ten sexual motives. They both seek intimacy, expression of love, mutual emotional feelings, marriage, to feel loved and to feel needed, according to a study by Elizabeth Allgeier at Bowling Green State University.

A n out of this world shared adventure

Tonight, share this with a lover and the heavens above.

Stars bright, stars light.
The first stars I see tonight.
Wishes were. Wishes might.
May all my wishes come true this night

Who says you can only have one wish on a starry night. My wish list is extensive and has become a list of dreams turned into realities. Your loving wish list can come true too. It has to start somewhere. Simon says, "Start it now."

One must learn to love, and go through a good
deal of suffering to get to it...
and the journey is always towards the other soul...

D.H. Lawrence

Flower power love – yes, it's true

Sticky Monkeyflower, mimulus aurantiacus–orange,
is a flower essence remedy that gently balances the
integration of sexual intimacy and human warmth. It nur-
tures your ability to express deep feelings of connectedness
and love, especially in loving sexual relationships.

What are flower essences? They are liquid plant prepa-
rations along the lines of homeopathic remedies. Using the
life force of the flowers, you can gently reorient and rebal-
ance the energy flows in your body. Food nourishes the
body. Flower essences nourish the soul. When used in con-
junction with powerful, positive thinking techniques, they
can greatly enhance your love life and relationships. Many
formulae exist. For further information and to order, here
are a few sources to contact:

- Flower Essence Services, P.O. Box 1769, Nevada
  City, CA 95959 Tel (916) 265-0258 in the U.S. & in
  Canada their toll free order line is 1 800 548-0075
- Pacific Essences, Box 8317, Victoria, B.C. V8W 3R9
  Canada
- Bach Flower Remedies, The Bach Centre, Mt.
  Vernon, Sotwell, Wallingford, Oxon 0X10 0PZ
  England
- Australian Bush Flower Essences 8A Oaks Avenue,
  Dee Why, NSW 2099 Australia
- Discover more flower power choices for emotional
  healing and growth in *Flower Remedies Handbook* by
  Donna Cunningham, Sterling Publishing Co.

Treat yourself to a facial, manicure or pedicure today

Good idea – treat your lover to one also.

Better idea – share the intimacy – both of you get facials, manicures and pedicures at the same time.

Best idea – Save money and create intimacy – Do a facial, manicure or pedicure for your lover. Then switch roles. Go for it — do all three at once for and with your lover. …Hey, guys, don't knock it until you try it. It's great fun!

Dong quai, a root, is used by Chinese herbalists in the treatment of female problems such as; PMS, hot flashes, menopause and vaginal dryness. It's said to have aphrodisiac properties in men and women since it enhances the effects of ovarian and testicular hormones. It may also build muscle tissue and enrich the blood. Check this out in *Prescription for Nutritional Healing*, by James Blanch, M.D. and Phyllis Balch, C.N.C, Avery Publishing Group. It is an extensive reference guide to drug-free remedies using minerals, herbs, vitamins and food supplements.

Quick tip sheet for super lovemaking...

Knowledge – what your physical and emotional needs are

Courage – to explore and be trusting and open with your partner

Freedom – to be yourself, authentic

Involvement – trust extended by both parties

Generosity – giving and getting in a balanced fashion

Communication – being open and non-judgmental about what another requests

Loving – context within which the experience takes place

Willingness – to seek help if you and your lover are experiencing problems. Willing to grow from the inside out.

Good health – keeping your body in working order and clean. Practicing safe sex.

Egalitarianism – both share equally in the experience

Sensuality – add a dash of romance and playfulness

Humor – laugh at yourself and enjoy the adventure.

Create the scent of love.

Romantic love sachets can add magic to your life.

Use a handful of dried herbs or plants as the filling for these sachets. Make the sachets out of 100% natural fiber material such as felt, wool or cotton, and choose an appro - priate color. Pink is best for love.

Cut the material into a square. Place the herb in the middle, gather ends and tie them tightly together. The size depend on where you want to put it.

You can put them in your closets or drawers. Occasionally, gently squeeze them to release the fragrance. Wear one. Put one in your purse if you choose. Use them in your car. Use them to attract love into your life.

To refresh a sachet, place it in a plastic bag and add drops of essential oils in the same ratio as the dried plant matter. Leave it in the bag overnight. The herbs should be replaced about every three months. Burying the used herbs returns them to the earth.

A romantic magical love sachet mixture – 3 parts lavender, 2 parts rose petals, 1 part orris root. Other plants you can use – orange petals, jasmine flowers, gardenia flowers, carnation petals. Sensual scents – olibanum, musk, saffron, jasmine, lilac, amber, indole and myrrh. It's okay to experiment to find the best formula for you.

Give the love sachet a boost. Use the power of your mind. Use this affirmation.

I'm a loving and caring person, who is attracting the same kind of person into my life.

Create Your Calendar of Romance

For each month of the year, assign a romantic theme, idea or activity. Here's a sample calendar. Copy it or create your own and then post it on the refrigerator or wall. ...Have fun.

Jan. – for the New Year – forgive past deeds – reaffirm your love for each other.

Feb. – Valentines Day – buy gift copies of the *For Lovers Only* series of books and audios – give them to friends and lovers as gifts.

Mar. – Spring – get potted flowers that grow well indoors.

Apr. – Get wet in the rain together.

May – Have a moonlight adventure.

June – Plan a sensual walk in nature – bring a bottle of wine and two wine glasses.

July – Do a romantic midnight picnic under the stars.

Aug. – Be kids for a day – neck at your local lovers leap.

Sept. – Share something about yourself that your lover didn't know – a fantasy, a fact, a fun thing you want to do – be imaginative.

Oct. – Dress as Cupid and Aphrodite for Halloween and pass out candy kisses to the neighborhood adults – Hershey's Kisses to the kids.

Nov. – Make a special romantic meal – use candles, take phone off the hook, dim the lights and lock the doors – order *Je T'aime* for Christmas gift giving – see below.

Dec. – Give each other sensual presents.

A unique gift is the audio cassette *Je T'aime (I Love You)*

which is the sensual sounds of a man and woman –
their moans, groans and purrs are set against a
backdrop of a babbling brook on side one, and
a babbling brook and the soothing sounds of
nature are on side two. Share it with your lover.

> I'm a dash biased since I created and produced it. Because of the
> soothing sensual resonance of my voice, many asked me to create
> this gift that I can now share with you. I have priced it at $9.95
> including taxes. I'll pay the delivery by mail if you tell them you
> read about it in this book. In North America, call toll free 1 800
> 263-1991, Overseas (519) 396-9553, fax (519) 396-9554.

Share the sensual textures of food

A dessert sampler with a difference — I call it the European sampler – a 'Little-of-Each.'
The next time you and friends come to the dessert part of your meal, each of you choose a different dessert. Prepare identical plates with small slices of every dessert on each plate.

Now the fun begins. Take turns closing your eyes and having someone put a forkful of a dessert in your mouth. What is very important is NOT to label a dessert by its proper name, but to describe: Textures – what the mouth feels. Tastes – sweet, sour, bitter, salty. Smell... Richness... Sharpness... of what you are tasting.

> Rediscover the wonder of tasting food for the first time

Be as descriptive as possible. Savor the simplicity and sensuousness of the moment. Move away from the desire to be right by trying to label the dessert. Labels by their very nature remove us from being in the moment and using our senses to the maximum. They dull the authenticity of an experience.

Savor the moment!

Trivia of the most important kind

Men have a monthly body rhythm, according to Dr. Alan Xenakis, that causes water retention, except the bloating is only one pint of fluid.

I guess that's why some women have PMS and some men have mental pause, where they think with a six inch brain.

Alternative health trivia of the most important kind

Discover a natural way to help reduce painful menstruation and the effects of menopause or morning sickness.

Homeopathy is one of the gentlest and safest forms of medical intervention. It is the first line of medical intervention in Europe and many other countries.

Sepia is a dried ink secretion of the Cuttlefish which is found near the Atlantic Ocean end of the Mediterranean Sea and in the North Sea. It is one of the oldest known gynecological remedies with no known side effects.

This is according to Dr. A. Vogel's *Swiss Guide to Homeopathic Medicines*. A. Vogel, a Swiss company has been pioneering natural choices since the mid 1900's. They use modern pharmaceutical production facilities and the finest ingredients. Their high quality natural products are available worldwide.

Trivia of the most important kind

According to researchers, the testosterone levels of men are at their highest in the morning. How about waking up early and having some morning delight?? Breakfast in bed, with a twist.

Women's love chemicals are highest at night.

31

Being driven crazy by what your lover is doing?

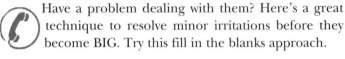 Have a problem dealing with them? Here's a great technique to resolve minor irritations before they become BIG. Try this fill in the blanks approach.

I feel _____ (label your feeling)

When you _____ (describe the annoying behavior)

Please _____ (suggest a suitable replacement behavior which is acceptable to you)

Here are a couple of examples…

I feel upset when you yell at me. Please lower your voice.

I feel frustrated when you leave your clothes lying on the couch. Please put them in the clothes hamper.

What makes this very effective is that you aren't using blame, guilt or other negative emotional statements. It is

> *LOWER*
> *LOWER*
> lower
> your voice

important that you take ownership of your feelings and become aware of them. Objectively state what behavior you do not want and most impor-tantly give a positive suggestion of acceptable behavior to replace that which bothered you.

Practice this, and you'll be amazed how those around you will start to slowly deal with situa-tions that may have become battle zones.

Point to ponder

"For the love of life…" is what this moment is about.

 Love must be relearned, and learned again, and again there is no end to it.

Katherine Porter

32

Natural lovemaking enhancer

Caviar, fish eggs, is a nutritious, rich source of protein. Their link with the reproductive process ties in with the myth of Aphrodite, the goddess of love born from sea foam. Anything from the sea sup - posedly shares Aphrodite's power.

A little rich for my tastes – maybe that's why it is so highly prized. Money, what it buys and what it symbolizes, is another form of aphrodisiac.

What's the recipe for a perfect marriage?

According to Linda and Pete, their secrets for a very happy marriage are:

We love each other dearly,
like each other very much, and have a lot of fun.

We offer ourselves to each other completely —
freely with trust and love.

Other's who know them say, "They adore each other and are very romantic – always!"

P.S. They got married at age 19 and 20, and just celebrated their 20th anniversary.

Share the energy,
with your lover or loving group.

Next time you are with a group of loving friends, sit in a circle facing one direction. Now the fun begins. Each of you massage the neck and back of the person in front of you. Focus on the caring that is uniting all of you. After ten minutes, turn around and massage the person who was massaging you. Continue doing this as long as you want.

Hawaiian Hugs

I created this type of hugging to gently combine touch and a yoga type of breathing to create a connection between two consenting people. It creates synchronicity as the energy flows are gently balanced between two people.

Step 1. Get the main ingredients – two consenting adults.

Step 2. Place your chests against each other, heart to heart.

Step 3. Firmly wrap your arms around each other.

Step 4. Breath in together, through your noses, inhaling deeply. Think of the air you inhale, as coming from heaven.

Step 5. Hold the breath in for a few seconds, then together, slowly release it through your mouths. Think of the exhale as going to the earth. You're blowing out all the junk from your mind and body.

Step 6. Repeat this breathing technique, at least three times before you release your partner.

Step 7. To enhance the affect of living in the moment, close your eyes after a few breaths.

Step 8. Continue hugging.

WARNING: If continued for extended periods, I cannot be held responsible for what happens. Please let me know if the result is a baby boy or baby girl.

FREE LOVE!?!

If romance is your game, buy a copy of *1001 Ways to Be Romantic* by Gregory Godek. If your book store cannot get it, you can order it from this toll free number 1 800 432-7444.

Gregory does Romance Seminars and has a fun newsletter full of creative, unusual and wonderful ideas, gifts and gestures, called the LoveLetter. To sign up for the newsletter, write LoveLetter, P.O. Box 226, Weymouth, Massachusetts 02188-0001

Currently, this $25 subscription newsletter is free for the asking. When you write them, tell them Ken Vegotsky, the speaker and author of *The Ultimate Power* and *222 Ways to Make Love With Life* sent you,  and they will waive the subscription cost. Do it soon. This is a time limited offer!

Natural lovemaking enhancer

 Eel is rich in phosphorus and has a chemical that excites the bladder. Its association to water and its phallic appearance foster this idea.

How do I love thee? Let me count the ways.
I love thee to the depth and breadth and height
My soul can reach, when feeling out of sight
For the ends of Being and ideal Grace
I love thee to the level of everyday's
Most quiet need, by sun and candle-light.
I love thee freely, as men strive for Right;
I love thee purely, as they turn from Praise.
I love thee with passion put to use
In my old griefs, and with my childhood's faith.
I love thee with a love seemed to lose
With my lost saint, – I love thee with the breath,
Smiles, tears, of all my life! – and if God choose,
I shall but love thee better after death.

Elizabeth Barret Browning

The giving of love is an education in itself.

Eleanor Roosevelt

Trivia of the love offering kind

Robert Browning, in 1847, discovered his wife, Elizabeth Barrett Browning had chronicled their growing friendship and love in her numerous sonnets — some of the greatest love poems of all time.

Unique expressions of the love offering kind

"Thoughts of love embolded me to bring this modest gift to the Jewish people...," said Marc Chagall, at the dedication of 12 stained-glassed windows he created for the Synagogue of the Hadassah-Hebrew University Medical Center in Jerusalem.

Now... create a unique gift for your lover.

There is always something left to love. And if you ain't learned that, you ain't learned nothing.

Lorraine Hansberry

Trivia of the important kind

What is the most important ingredient in a relation - ship? "LOVE," you say? Dr. Zick Rubin of Brandeis University surveyed one thousand men. They were asked, "If you were single and a potential mate had all the qualities you desire, would you marry them, even if you weren't in love?"

The overwhelming response, reports *First,* was "No!" Zick found that 65% said love is more important than per - sonality, physical attractiveness or looks.

Trivia of the most interesting kind

"Matchmaker, matchmaker make me a $1,000,000 match..."

Do you want to marry a world class Mr./Ms. Right!? Do you have a friend in need? Now's your chance to do a good deed. It's FREE!

Mate-Search International charges it's rich and famous clients $10,000 for ten matches. Business tycoons, professional athletes, sheiks, movie stars, socialites, etcetera use this one of a kind service.

They found a husband for a famous movie star, a wife for a Saudi Sheik, a husband for a best selling romance novelist, a wife for a prominent law school dean – just to name a few. To date, the results are 19 marriages, 17 engagements and 18 cohabitations.

The average Joe or Josephine can get into their database-of-love for FREE! How?

Send three photos, a work resume and a biographical sketch to Robert Davies & Associates, Mate-Search International, 2024 Stone Ridge Lane, Villanova, Pennsylvania 19085. It's that simple!

TIP.   Got a spare $10,000 and want to find your perfect match, call Robert at 610-527-6749.

P.S.   Robert, I'm sending you a copy of this book, three photos, work resume and biography as soon as it is published. That is unless I get very lucky and/or have a spare $10,000 kicking around.

To save a little time here's a sketch of my bio:
Single – Divorced after 17 years married to a very fine lady.
Two great kids.
Birthday – December 18, 1951.
For presents I accept cash, charge cards, gifts and plain old best wishes.
Sign – Sagittarius.
Hobbies – loves walks in woods, candlelight moments, hugs and kisses, living in the moment. Loves people.

Down to earth – I don't feel the need or desire to dress up pre-ferring to be very very comfortable.

Experimental cook – in other words my mistakes become soup.

Work – Author, professional speaker and entrepreneur alias professional mischief maker.

Income – Roller coaster style.

Physical features – Heavyset alias cuddly. Five foot six and a half inches. Left arm partially paralyzed, collapsed lung. Full head of dark brown hair with a sprinkling of gray.

Stench of humor, I'd say. Others say I have a sense of humor.

Favorite hobby – Making Love With Life!

L ove is, above all, the gift of oneself.

Jean Anouilh

W hich came first, the chicken or the egg? Who cares? But if your looking for a scientifically proven aphrodisiac, then go for fertilized hens egg, spe-cially formulated and mixed with natural ingredi-ents in a powder form, called Ardor or Libido.

It was discovered by Dr. Bjodne Eskeland of Norway while researching far eastern sexual stimulants. In Norway, 83% of men in a double blind study reported results ranging up to "a very pronounced increase" in sex drive. Women appear to also benefit from Ardor.

The New York Academy of Science recently introduced it to the North American marketplace. Major research studies are under way. It has been found to counteract the loss of sex drive experienced with anti-depressants such as Prozac. Excellent results indicated Ardor eliminated this frustrating problem. It works for many men and women. The product contains no cholesterol and has no known side effects. Phewww...

TIP: Ask your doctor to get the studies or prescribe it for you. In the USA call 1 800 446-0778 – In Canada call 1 888 667-2677 – Overseas can fax (416) 537-5806.

Hot Tip — Forbidden knowledge

Ardor might be a cure for some cancers, or at the very least, it's been shown to help stop certain types of cancers from spreading!

Dr. John Ralston Davidson of Winnipeg, Manitoba, Canada, during the 1940's, injected a liquid from fertilized chicken eggs along with dietary supplementation to help cancer patients. The medical establishment refused to fund or support his inexpensive cancer treatment.

Hundreds were saved, including a politician, under Dr. Davidson's care. The politician tried to get the Canadian Prime Minister to give the doctor funding. All attempts and pleas by parties whose lives were saved or improved by the cancer treatment were stonewalled.

In 1997, a top rated T.V. news show broadcast this story. Avis Favaro, a medical and health specialist reporter and Ingrid Kreisel, researcher, were instrumental in bringing this to the public's attention.

Love is Patient, Love is kind,
it does not envy; it does not boast; it is not proud.
It is not rude, it is not self-seeking,
it is not easily angered, it keeps no record of wrongs.
Love does not delight in evil
but rejoices with the truth. It always protects,
always trusts, always hopes, always perseveres.

I Corinthians 13:4-7

Sex is certainly one of the expressions of love, but love itself has nothing to do with sex. Love is devotion to the destiny of the one loved. And love is joy: joy in the spirit, joy in the soul and joy in the body.

Alan Howard, *Sex in the Light of Reincarnation and Freedom,*
St. George Press

39

Trivia of the rush kind... More chemistry of love

By now you've embraced oxytocin, a love chemical. Two other chemicals that create a natural high are endorphins and seritonin. Endorphins cause a run - ners high. When you make love, you release these chemicals, at different states of being. Oh what a rush it is! They heal. They help. There isn't anything like them.

How to access love anywhere — anytime — anyplace

Love is in the air. Stephanie, my daughter, was four years old when she helped me discover this powerful tech - nique. I was leaving for work when she blew me a kiss.

Seeing this, I stopped the car... got out... reached up into the air to grasp her homeless kiss in my hand. Then I slapped my cheek, planting her kiss on it. Next I blew her a kiss. She caught on pretty quickly, reaching up, catching my kiss then slapping her face. Then she blew me back another kiss. I caught it and placed it on my cheek. It was a volleyball game of kisses.

Throwing kisses and catching kisses, is one of the safest ways to access the love that surrounds us each and every day.

Trivia of the love kind

Can you name the planet of love?
Hint: It's the only planet not named after
     a Greek or Roman deity.
        Give up?

Answer: Venus

The chemistry of love continued

Why do women want to hug and cuddle more then men do? They have a higher base amount of oxytocin.

Massage and physical touch are what produce this love chemical. When a woman gives birth, her levels of oxytocin are 3 to 5 times greater than usual. Allopathic doctors (medicine as practiced just in the last century) use oxytocin to induce labor. At higher concentrations, it causes uterine contractions to start. Think of oxytocin as the first domino and nature takes care of itself.

> P.S. Men and women produce more oxytocin when they are massaged and caressed. It helps lower blood pressure and promotes other healing aspects of human physiology. Is this what is meant by a natural high?
>
> Quick - hug me - now! …Aaaahhhhh… Thanks.

Be a kid again

On a rainy day, go puddle jumping.

"Remember to wear an old pair of shoes or rubbers."
Does that sound like someone you know

Shared memories —
They are what love and romance are all about.

# Audio to put you and a lover in the mood,
for loving and living in the moment:

- *Canto Gregorian Chants* by Benedictine Monks. EMI Records. Repetitive sound of monks chanting that soothes and cleanses the mind. You can order it through your local record store.
- *Temba African Tapestries* by Hennie Bekker. African rhythms with a powerful sensual undercurrent. To

41

order call The Nature Loft at (905) 773-6848 ask for their catalog. Hennie's music is incredible.

– *Intimacy: Music for Love* by Raphael. Hearts of Space. Orchestrated music of passion and beauty. Available in stores. To order in North America, call Music Design toll free 1 800 862-7232, (www.hos.com)

– *Je t'aime* (I love you) created by Ken Vegotsky, AGES Publications. Sensually erotic lovers moans and groans with a background of natural sounds such as a babbling brook and rushing water. Playful and fun to get you in the mood. Not available in retail outlets. In North America to order call toll free 1 800 263-1991, Overseas (519) 396-9553.

P.S.   I am not related to Hennie, Raphael or the Benedictine Monks.

I Love to touch you... I touch to Love you."

Sharon Warren, *Angel Fingerprints*

 T rivia of the most important kind.

The toe has more nerve endings than the other anatomical parts most people associate with love - making. So next time you step on it, remember toes can be the source of great pleasure – in more ways than one!

F inancial success can be accomplished with 25% planning, 25% timing, 25% working, 25% waiting — or by marrying someone who is already wealthy.

Author Unknown

Keys to diffuse tension

Active listening skills are one of the best ways to diffuse tension and the accompanying stress. Here are keys to putting them into practice with a partner.

Stop what your doing – all activities. Make your posture physically inviting, open to receiving. Make direct eye contact.

Show your interested using facial expressions. Encourage the speaker nonverbally as well as verbally.

Identify the content of the persons message. Identify their feelings and unstated messages.

Clarify what you heard. Paraphrase what was said. Verify what you heard.

Hugs — vitamins for your mind-body-soul connection.

Hugs add quality to your life as well as offering gentle healing. I see cuddles and hugs as the origin of therapeutic touch.

Your hugging needs may vary from mine. Use my daily hug chart as a guideline to discover your hug quotient.

Ken's Daily Hug Chart

3 hugs a day for minimal sustenance of self. It leaves you thirsty.

6 hugs a day for nurturing. You feel quenched but still unsatisfied.

9 hugs a day for regular growth. Feels good.

12+ hugs a day for inner, outer and spiritual growth. It stores some away for those occasional hugging lapses. Your mind-body-soul will know this.

Excerpt from *The Ultimate Power: How To Unlock Your Mind-Body-Soul Potential,* Ken Vegotsky, AGES Publications

Chocolate covered Strawberries

It's the chocolate that does it. Chocolate produces PEA (amphetamine-like phenylethylamine). Peoples bodies produce this when they are attracted to each other. It creates a euphoric mood of optimism and happiness, which also happens when falling in love. Have chocolates before that loving moment. Using choco - late as body paint is another possibility. Let your imagination run wild!

Three erotic massage techniques

Kneading, Gliding and Spider Walking are the three main ways you can sensually massage another or yourself. Variations on a theme can be even more exciting. By com - bining and using all three techniques, you'll discover that different parts of the body react differently to the various types of touch. Each individual has their own preferences. Part of the fun is exploring and discovering what they are. There are numerous books on massage. I prefer Swedish massage for sensuality – the only problem is you melt.

Use massage oils, preferably with 100% pure botanical essential oils in them. A mixture I love to share with a partner includes the essential oils of ylang-ylang, san - dalwood, frankincense and bay, mixed into a base of safflower and almond organic oils. Very little is needed for total coverage as these oils go a long way. They also nourish the skin and body.

The best premixed massage oil containing these ingre - dients that I found is the Aromaforce™ line distributed by BioForce. Experiment and find out what works best for you. Aromatherapy massage is an incredibly beneficial way to enhance your wellbeing. Combine massage with inner physical healing and the accompanying excitement is a romantic and loving combination that you and your partner can share.

No partner? That's okay. Nurture and massage your own body. You'll enjoy and languish in the sense of self-discovery and fulfillment. Take a bath and put an ounce of the oil in the tub, your skin will feel silky smooth and deliciously delightful afterwards. Your mind and body will love it.

Lovemaking 101

Sex expert Sari Locker, author of *Mindblowing Sex In The Real World,* shares these four quick tips:

1) Be in the moment, by taking care of all distracting problems like the phone and protection first.
2) Use the five physical senses – Taste, touch, smell, sight and hearing – when lovemaking.
3) Variety and experimentation are okay.
4) Learn how to pleasure yourself.

ADD this idea to the list.

Find a place where you and your partner can lovingly communicate your wants, needs and desires. Make it a safe place free of distraction or concern for interruption. Listen and share with each other, without passing judgment, as you explore the intimate side of your physical and emotional well being.

A natural high that really works

A natural high!? Intoxicated by any perfumes or manly aftershaves lately? Pheromones, a sexually stimulating by-product of the human body, enhance frequency of love - making. In the USA and Canada, designer or store brands such as *Realm* by Erox Corporation are using a synthetic replica of the human hormone. They are selling briskly in major department stores. Now I wonder why?

> To order you can write to Erox Corporation, 4034 Clipper Court, Fremont, California 94538. In a rush in the USA and Canada call toll free 1 888 777-3256, Overseas call (510) 226-6874.

> TIP: You'll find another pheromone derivative product later on. It's different – remember buyer be savvy.

Consumer beware!

'Spanish fly' is an extract from the Spanish blister beetle technically named the canthradides. It causes extreme irritation to the urogenital tract, in addition to numerous other bad symptoms.

Sometimes it is sold as 'Spanish Fly Placebo' or another such name. Placebo means a harmless unmedicated prepa - ration given as medicine, usually to humor the recipient. Save your money. Go out for a romantic evening instead.

Be a kid again

Share the experience with a lover. Put your toes in sand, whipped cream or try a Jello bath.

Discover a wonderful book

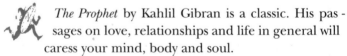 *The Prophet* by Kahlil Gibran is a classic. His pas - sages on love, relationships and life in general will caress your mind, body and soul.

Add romance to an outing. Find a park or natural set - ting. Read passages from *The Prophet* to your lover and have them choose a passage to read to you.

Quick stress reducing techniques that can help get you revved up for lovemaking with life or a partner

Stress causes blood to flow toward the limbs from the central body and sexual organs. This can result in a reduced sex drive as well as a loss of pleasure in making love with life. To reduce the affects of stress, try these quick methods.

Drink water. Stress causes sweating which leads to feeling dehydrated. Drink at least two glasses of water at bed - time and you'll feel better.

Straighten yourself out. Many people slouch when they are stressed which reduces blood flow and restricts breathing. Sitting up straight helps you breath easier and get more life enhancing oxygen into your brain.

Deep breathing. Press your palms against your legs or each other. Keep a steady pressure on your hands and take a deep breath through your nose and hold it in for five seconds. Slowly exhale through your mouth, and at the same time, let your hands relax. Repeat this five to ten times, stopping once you feel relaxed.

TIP: Great before lovemaking or anytime you need to boost your life force energy.

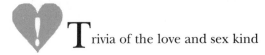 Trivia of the love and sex kind

The act of making love, using the western concepts of sex, burns up 150 calories, according to researchers. Now if toning up or losing weight is your aim, discover how surfing the orgasm can burn a lot more calories in a deli - ciously delightfully fulfilling way for the both of you.

I'm not going to make it easy, but here's a hint – the ancient Chinese courts discovered the power of the rule of nine, thousands of years ago. I hope you enjoy your journey through this book to discover

47

what this technique is about. It's simple and if you try it you'll be very happy.

Love, like sex, should be savored. Enjoy the journey and think of this as mental foreplay. Teasing also can be fun.

Trivia of the sweetest kind

The only food that does not spoil is honey. Archeological digs have turned up totally edible honey in ancient tombs, thousands of years old.

So the next time you call your partner *Honey,* tell them it's because you feel love transcends time.

Isn't that a sweet idea.

(This last comment was put in to help you practice the art of love talk - moaning and groaning.)

Trivia of the least important kind

A poll reported in *Redbook* asked couples:

Would you lend out your spouse for a night for a million dollars?

"No way," said two out of three.
"I'd consider it and give it some thought," replied 16%.
"It's a deal," said one out of ten.

Wine with class

Cleopatra prepared an opulent banquet for Mark Anthony. In a glass of wine, she put two invaluable pearls. Then toasting his health, she downed the con - coction of pearls and wine. Cleopatra insisted her tribute to Mark Anthony exceed the feasts cost. It did.

Once they became lovers, Mark Anthony presented Cleopatra with gifts for her empire: Phonecia, Cyprus, Cilicia, Judea, Coele-Syria, and parts of Arabia.

A natural romance enhancer that really works

Pheromones with a difference from the co-discoverer Winnifred Cutler. She is an American biologist and wellness guru who co-discovered pheromones in humans in 1986. A study she did in the 1990's found that forty-seven percent of men who used a pheromone laced aftershave reported having more sex, while only nine percent of those using a placebo laced aftershave reported having more sex. Similar results were found for women.

Other researchers have discovered that men and women feel a greater degree of comfort and relaxation when using products with the appropriate pheromones for their gender. They greatly enhanced their love lives.

How do you get the them? Write to Winnifred Culter at The Athena Institute, 1211 Braefield Rd., Chester Springs, Pennsylvania 19425. It is staffed with health care professionals and supplies scientifically studied pheromones – one for men, another for women. To get information or order call (610) 827-2200.

Pricey but effective. A small bottle lasts three to four months. According to the testimonials it really works!

> TIP: Businesses are marketing animal derived pheromone based products. They do not appear to have the same aphrodisiac qualities of the human variety. If not sure, keep on shopping. Buyer beware! Buyer be happy!

Trivia of the least important kind

All things are not as they seem. Too often we base the acceptance of things on their titles, names or labels. This applies to our acceptance of sexual activities and loving relationships just as it applies to the title of a book. Here are two that may surprise you.

Blossom and the Flower became *Peyton Place.*
Tomorrow is Another Day became *Gone With the Wind.*

What do many Russians do during those cold winter nights? They warm up by reading a copy of one of the great romance novels of all time, *Dr. Zhivago* by Boris Leonidovich Pasternack. Get the video and watch it with your partner.

The joy of self-loving

Dr. Betty Dodson, a noted sex-therapist, created a straightforward appealing guidebook that reveals satisfying ways to explore your sexual nature. Demonstrated in a warm, intelligent fashion, it's suitable for both men and women. Self-love, more than just a physical process, is a way of lovingly affirming your life and human experience.

Interested? Yes! The book is *Sex for One*, by Betty Dodson, Ph.D., Crown Trade Paperbacks. Get a copy for yourself or for anyone whom you believe may want to explore this intimate side of themselves.

Share this poem with a lover

Now you feel no Rain,
for each of you will be shelter for the other.
Now you will feel no cold,
for each of you will be warmth for the other.
Now there is no more loneliness,
for each of you will be companion to the other.
Now you are two persons,
but there is only one life before you.
Go now to your dwelling,
to enter into the days of your life together.
And may your days be good
and Long upon the earth.

American Indian Wedding Prayer

Loving technique to connect to the moment

Whenever you feel distracted in life or during love-making, try this. Breath and say to yourself the following:

I breath in and connect to my mind-body-soul...

I breath out and smile... Living in the moment... This is the only moment...

I breath in and connect to my mind-body-soul...

Keep repeating this until your mind is cleared of chatter. Time your breathing with the thoughts. Continue repeating while you focus on your breathing. Feel the life affirming oxygen caressing your lungs. Savor the sensations. Let your worries and distractions melt away with each breath.

Closing your eyes will deepen the relaxation. This works great in times of stress, lovemaking and whenever you want a powerful way to connect to the moment. Trust yourself. The rewards are incredible. Start now, for a few minutes.

This is my expansion of an ancient meditation from the Far East. In modern terms, it can also cause the relaxation response to manifest itself.

 Love is the aphrodisiac of life.

Romantic morning adventure

Take a little time the evening before to prepare a light picnic basket for an early morning adventure. Go to sleep early, or just set your alarm clock to wake you up before sunrise.

Get up and go to it — take blankets and your bundle of breakfast delights to the front or backyard or to the place you first necked if it's not too far a drive. Savor the sunrise together, arm in arm or nestled in each others arms.

Add a dash of romantic background music such as Raphael's wonderful albums on the Sound Designs label, classical music or the theme from Space Odyssey 2001 as the sun rises before your eyes.

TIP: Got kids, get up early enough so you can have a fresh start to the day. Savor the silence, your breakfast and share a sunrise cuddle session.

Laughter is an aphrodisiac for love.

So are hot bagels and cream cheese shared at sunrise.

Erotic and easy dessert – Frozen Grapes

Ingredients: Grapes - as many as you want.
Separate the grapes from the vine. Wash and gently pat them dry. About an hour before you want to eat them, put them in a freezer safe container and pop them into the freezer.

TIP: Seedless grapes are best for this, but I prefer grapes with seeds. Why? The seeds contain a powerful healing chemical, that is released when you chew on them. The technical name for the active ingredient is 'proantho - canidins'... Now that is a mouthful!

Give a boost to your desires

Hormone replacement therapy for women, and now men, is a growing field. The testosterone patch is restoring the sex lives of men with flagging sex drive. It also appears to enhance their sense of well being.

Similar therapies using testosterone alone or with estrogen are being tested for women. See your doctor if you want to examine this option.

Trivia of the 'picture this' kind

Do women get aroused by porno films? According to Ellen Laan, a Dutch psychologist and researcher, yes.

Using genital blood flow measurements, physiologically women were just as aroused as men. The difference was that women said they were repelled and disgusted by the standard male orientated sex films, yet porno films made female friendly aroused them.

The orgasm and arousal gap appears to not be physi - cally but mentally based. This suggests society's messages and cultural views about sex have a major bearing on how women see themselves and their sexual side. Becoming aware of the hidden and discreet negative mes - sages our culture creates about female sexuality is a step toward liberating oneself from them.

Realization and awareness are keys for con - sciously and successfully tapping into your sexual nature, to liberating yourself and living your life to the fullest.

Maybe... Maybe Not

'Yohimbine', which comes from the bark of the Pausinystalia johimbe (yohimbe tree) of tropical West Africa, is used for enhancing sexual function. The isolated alkaloid, yohimbine hydrochloride, from this herb appears to have some potent effects on sexual func - tion. Its primary action is to increase erectile tissue blood flow, thereby helping to increase libido.

CAUTION: The FDA has approved it as a drug. Numerous side effects have been noted such as anxiety, panic attacks, hallucinations, effects on the cardiovascular system, increased blood pressure, skin flushing, and headaches. It is definitely not recommended for those with psychological problems or kidney disease and should not be used by pregnant women.

Only use under the care of a doctor until further studies and evidence are made available to the public. There are numerous other safer natural alternatives you'll discover between the covers – of this book.

Practice the art of mutual meditation

Meditation, yoga, Zen — they all work by inducing what Dr. Herbert Benson, of Harvard Medical School's interna - tionally acclaimed Mind/Body Clinic, calls the relaxation response.

"This phenomenon shuts off the distracting, stressful, anxiety producing aspects of what is commonly called the 'fight-or-flight' response," Dr. Benson writes in his book *Your Maximum Mind*.

It is one of the best ways to clear and cleanse your mind, body and soul. It helps you gain a greater awareness of body sensations, thoughts, feelings and most importantly, loving kindness.

Here's a quick way to access the power of meditation.

1) Pick a word or phrase to focus on – for example *love* or *magic* or *peace*. It must be firmly part of your belief system.
2) Find a safe place and sit quietly, close your eyes and relax.
3) Each time you exhale, start repeating your focus word or phrase. Synchronize this with your breathing.
4) Continue for 10 to 30 minutes.

Do this once a day. How you're doing it is not as important as just doing it. If thoughts distract you, return to the word or phrase and continue.

You and your lover can share this time together. Mutual meditation, this shared experience, can produce what I call the state of harmonious synchronicity.

An incredible video you and your lover can repeatedly share, in the privacy of your home, is *The Inner Art of Meditation* as demonstrated by Jack Kornfield Ph. D., therapist and meditation instructor. It is produced by Sounds True Audio of Boulder, Colorado. The price is well worth it. Sharing the journey together will be a delightful experience, increasing your ability to live fully in the moment as you make love – with life.

To order this video in North America call toll free 1 800 333-9185 Overseas call (303) 449-6229 or fax (303) 665-5292. Ask for their catalog of audio and video products. You'll be glad you did.

Excerpt from *Stress Free Living: 222 Ways to Live Stress Free & Make Love With Life*, Ken Vegotsky, AGES Publications

Attract love into your life
with a loving herb bath formula

It's cheap, easy and fun to create.

You make a sachet out of herbs, using a piece of torn hosiery, cheesecloth or an old face cloth. The mesh should be fine enough to hold the herbs inside the sack.

Think of the tub as a giant tea pot in which you brew your homemade tea. When put in warm water, herbs release their energies, scents and colors. Give the sachet time to release it's essence in the water. You'll smell the scent and see the color when the bath is ready.

Baths are powerful tools to release personal psy - chic powers and draw love into your life. Here's an ancient formula the wise women healers of long ago used:

Herb Love Bath –   3 parts Rose petals,
                   2 parts Lovage, 1 Part Dill

Other herbs you may want to try in combination are Rosemary, Lavender, Cardamom, Orange flowers, Gardenia petals and Ginger... to name a few.

TIP: Premixed Love Teas exist. Check them out and throw them in the tub.

To maximize the benefits of the love bath, repeat the baths in the morning and evening. Visualize yourself as being a caring and loving person who is seeking someone of like mind. This helps manifest love in your life.

Got a lover, then share the bath, strengthen your bonds and savor the experience.

H ave an eye opener of an experience.

Many men and women close their eyes during sex to focus on the physical sensations of lovemaking. This shuts them off from their partners. Next time, look into your partners eyes. It will not take away from the physical plea - sure, but it will make the experience more intimate.

 P oint to ponder.

Man is the only animal that blushes. Or needs to.

Mark Twain

T rivia of the most interesting kind

A recent survey, conducted in shopping malls across America, found these were the favorite pet names used by men for their women:

Sweet Cheeks	Honey	Honey Bear
Sweetie	Sweatpea	Babe
Snuggle Bunch	Lover	Snookums

These are the nicknames women used for their men:

Honey	Pooky	Honey Bear
Babe	Pumpkin	Sugar
Honey Bunch	Darling	Dude

Lovemaking — one of the oldest healing arts

Dr. Mariam Stoppard, author of *The Magic of Sex*, notes a physiological benefit of sexual arousal is a stronger immune system. In addition, the circulating levels of hormones and endorphins increase. So, people feel better and heal faster.

The benefits to women are quite extensive. A renewed sense of well being and acknowledgement of their inner beauty, in this fashion, is physically, emotionally and spiritually nourishing. After menopause, a slight increase in testosterone levels often produces a heightened sense of physical need.

Interestingly as men age, sexual release can have a positive affect upon enlarged prostates. This should be of particular interest to men over age 40, the age after which prostate problems usually start occurring. The prostate is intimately connected with the urological functioning of the male body. A healthy prostate is important to sexual potency and the ability to urinate. Saw Palmetto and pumpkin seeds are two natural things that help the prostate function better.

Women's cycles are also enhanced by botanical sources. Evening Primrose oil contains important essential fatty acids, which help alleviate the effects of premenstrual syndrome (PMS). This is natures way of making love with humans – by supplying our bodies with life and love enhancing nutrients.

I mention this to make you aware of the subtle, yet essential nature of our fragile existence and partnership with the planet. Honor the earth and it will repay you in kind.

When love and skill work together, expect a masterpiece.

John Ruskin

Be an animal

When you're alone, practice pleasuring yourself and create your own moaning and groaning symphony. When you're ready, gently introduce your symphony to your lover during lovemaking and discover their reactions.

You're gently guiding them to your hot spots.

Become a generous lover

Turn off that radio station in your head called W.I.I.F.M. (What's In It For Me). Turn on the lovers radio station W.I.I.F.M.P. (What's In It For My Partner).

P.S.   It is also OK to be selfish and request what pleases you. The key is balance and harmony.

Creativity… a powerful way to unlock your love life

A starter technique, to help release your higher cre - ative powers, is called morning pages. This is my simplified starter version.

1) Put a pen and paper by your night table.
2) First thing when you get up in the morning, write down whatever comes into your head. If you cannot think of anything, write *I cannot think of anything* until you fill up one page. Don't let your inner censor stop you from writing whatever you want. There is no right or wrong content. Think of it as exercising and stretching your creativity muscle. It is not a diary, but a way of reflecting your thoughts.
3) Fill up one page for a start. Then work your way up to three pages a day.

4) Be creative. You and your lover can share the beauty of discovering how to express your inner selves by using this idea.

Whether you focus on just uncovering that inner cre - ative genius every person has, or writing wild, sensual, zany, erotic, romantic or whatever you wish ideas, the important point is that you liberate yourself from your inner critic. Finding your authentic voice helps you become better in tune with yourself. In turn, a more fulfilled person becomes a better sharing companion with their lover.

> TIP: A great book to help you understand and discover your higher creative self is the *The Artists Way* by Julia Cameron, The Putnam Berkeley Group. Available in bookstores or to order it toll free call 1 800 788-6262

Savor the sensual electricity of one of the twentieth centuries most highly acclaimed female authors of erotic books for women – Anais Nin. She was said to have started writing the stories for her husband, to keep him happy and their marriage monogamous. Eventually, she created books from them. Her husband was Hugh Guiler who wrote under the name of Ian Hugo.

Anais Nin's writings have been described as surreal dreams of a poetic nature that are mysteriously intriguing. Her erotic writings do not use any language that one would call explicit, in the negative sense.

> It's amazing what can happen between the covers
> – of a great book!!!
> What do you think I meant anyhow?

Write your lover an erotic and romantic story. Share it with them, then... Imagination – it is such a wonderful gift. Use yours today.

Ladies, share Anais Nin's books with your lover. It's a

great way for creating understanding and mutual respect for different perceptions of reality.

Men, buy a copy for your lover and read it. Many ladies told me they read only her works – they swore by them.

Mind expanding idea: Looking for adult fiction? Try bookstores and libraries under Erotica, Sexuality, Relationships, Fiction, Self-help… Use your imagina-tion and enjoy the adventure. Make it an inexpen-sive outing – take your lover and both of you search for the best five titles you would like to share. Then grab a secluded spot and decide on the one from each pile you want to buy and take home with you to read and share with each other.

Give all to love, obey thy heart.

Ralph Waldo Emerson

Alternative health love enhancer

Muira puama (Ptychopetalum olacoides) is a little known exotic herb that recent French studies indicate improved sexual functioning with some patients. It is from a Brazilian shrub. Dr. Jacques Waynberg did the study through the Institute of Sexology in Paris. He is one of the world's leading author-ities on sexual functioning.

A significant number of subjects involved in the study derived benefits from this herb. No negative side effects were discovered. The active ingredient(s) and how it works are not yet known.

Synergistic blends are formulae combining many dif-ferent nutrients. Synergy means the effect of two or more components is greater than that of any single one. The complexity of studying the interactions of the individual parts and human physiology is one that researchers have great difficulty doing. Things work, yet we don't necessarily have to know why to utilize them. The universe works. Our understanding of why is not necessary to its functioning. It just does. Accepting this and gently trying to apply the gifts of our world is what making love with life is about.

Masculex (Enzymatic therapy) is a synergistic blend used by Dr. Julian Whitaker at his Wellness Institute in Newport Beach, California. It contains Muira puama, Ginkgo biloba, Panax ginseng, and nutri - ents for enhanced sexual functioning such as zinc, liver extract, beta-sitosterol, saw palmetto and wheat germ oil.

N o space
No time
Separate
Two Souls
Forever joined
in Universal Love

Sharon Warren
from *One Light One Love*

E nrich your life

Before you go to bed tonight, list five things for which you are truly grateful. They can be the simplest of things – a roof over your head, a warm bed to sleep in, clean water, food, a smile you put on some ones face, the simple fact that you are alive.

Reconnect to the wonder of being alive. Do it each and every night. Take nothing for granted – especially your lover.

P.S. Say a little prayer for this to become a kinder, gentler and more loving world. Every thought counts.

Each moment embraced in the arms of love
is as sacred as that which goes before it and
that which comes after it.

Lovemaking technique from the Ancient Hebrews

According to one of their 613 Mitzvot
– precepts or rules of conduct for ones life –
a husband is obligated to first sexually please his
wife before he does himself.

This ancient wisdom reflects what science and sexolo -
gists are discovering is one of the keys for improving one's
love life.

The course of true love never did run smooth.

William Shakespeare

Try this five step plan for easier
conflict resolution and a better love life

1) Keep sex separate from non-sexual problems. If you're
   angry, don't use sex as a way of expressing the anger.
   The signals are too confusing.
2) Deal with one problem at a time.
3) Clearly define what the problem is.
4) Use creative thinking to brainstorm solutions. List
   everything – there are no right or wrong answers at this
   point, just an exploration of possibilities. One idea
   leads to another and so on and so on.
5) Clarify the issue. Summarize it and come to a final
   agreement. Be willing to put the agreement on paper.

Key to this whole process — a willingness to compromise.
Reconciliation works wonders.

Enrich your relationships

Practice forgiveness and thankfulness daily. They go hand-in-hand making life a more loving experience.

The Tao of lovemaking and romance

This is a Far Eastern system that stresses male ejaculatory control. It was created in China to enhance the level of satisfaction for men and women in their physical, emotional and spiritual relationships.

One key is strong pelvic muscles, in the pubococcygeal muscle group, called the PC muscles. Strengthening this muscle group in men and women can significantly increase thesexual pleasure and leads to better, deeper and more prolonged orgasms. Another key is the rule of nine – the suggestion that the state of mutual arousal is maintained longer when men never thrust deeply more than nine times in a row.

Tip: To explore this beautiful way of sharing and love making, read *The Tao of Love and Sex: The Ancient Chinese Way to Ecstasy,* by Jolan Chang, Penguin Books.

Morning madness – of the heart warming kind

Breakfast in (or out of) bed will never be the same. This is for the gentlemen lovers or vice versa. It doesn't matter. The key is that you just do it!

The setting: Dim lighting with soft music – classical, opera, nature sounds, new age – in the background, flowers or a plant moved temporarily into the bedroom. One stays in bed as the other gets into mischief as they create this special moment. Anticipation can be very sensual. Let your imagination run wild.

Apparel: Whatever you want. Nothing is good enough for you and your lover. *(Damn, I love a good pun.)*

Ambience plus: Laugh, giggle, get a big feather and...

The menu: Pop Pillsbury croissant, cinnamon or dinner roll dough into the oven. The aroma is intoxicating. Let bake while you're serving the first treat, a cup of freshly brewed exotic coffee – just add a dash of cinnamon, vanilla, or almond on top of the grinds before the water drips through – or substitute a glass of fresh juice. Twinning's and Celestial Seasonings make wonderful exotic regular and herb teas, try one for a change. Honey, lemon and milk. Serve on a nice tray or an ugly one covered with nice linen or a pillowcase.

Presentation is everything – well almost.

Cook things that you know how to make. Add a dash of style to it in the presentation. Cut up a few sprigs of parsley, it cleans the breath and is chock full of healthy nutrients. The key is to enjoy the moment and each other. Pace yourself. Leisurely enjoy every minute, every second, every moment.

By now the aroma of fresh baked goods should be whet - ting your appetites, awakening your senses.

Rather than cooking lots of things, be lazy and be healthy. Create a basket of ripe fresh fruit resting on a bed of lettuce or a napkin. Using canned fruits is okay when served in bowls or on plates. Get a couple of fresh exotic fruits like mango, kiwi, strawberries, raspberries, blueber - ries, watermelon – whatever is in season.

Add a pitcher of cool water and two wine glasses. Don't forget a knife, plate and a bunch of grapes... Grapes!? Yes! Peel one slowly, and gently pop it into your lovers waiting mouth. Don't rush. Savor.

Keep discovering the little pleasures that mean so much. Sometimes, you have to tease before you please.

HOT IDEA: Be playful, use your lovers tummy or nooks and crannies as a table. Pretend it's a bread roll, put honey on it. On your mark ... get set... nibble away.

TIP: Schedule a time next month, where you reverse roles. Variety really is the spice of life, love and romance. Who says dates have to be in the evening anyhow?

Afternoon delight

Play hooky during the week. That's right! You heard me. Whatever you and your lover normally do during a week day afternoon – be it work, take the kids to an activity, shop, clean house, see clients... — DON'T DO IT! STOP! — Play hooky.

You and your lover deserve to take a time out with each other. Breaking old patterns helps establish new and exciting opportunities. Be creative... Have fun... just like you did when you skipped school.

TIP: Feeling guilty? Then think of it as a mental health day. I call them *sanity breaks*. They help you focus on what really matters – moving you from a state of doing to one of being... being fully in the moment.

Loving, like prayer, is a power as well as a process. It's curative. It is creative.

Zona Gale

Improve your love life with a Live Loving and Love Living journaling experience

Become your own best friend. Discover a mental breath of fresh air. Use journaling to create better self-awareness.

How? You write letters to yourself about your feelings, thoughts, activities and ideas.

The benefits of this process include: greater self-aware-ness, organization of thoughts, problem solving and setting attainable goals. In addition, your writing and communica-tion skills improve.

65

Getting started is easy. Get a spiral note pad or fancy bound book with blank pages. Next, sit down and write. Spelling and grammar are not important. Let your creative juices flow. Don't censor yourself. This is your gift to your - self.

A great opening is today's date. Then write... Dear Self. I end all my letters with... Love, Ken. For the best results write anytime, anywhere and often. This is a portable activity. A private and quiet place is recommended, but not necessary. Express your feelings in writing by noting that you are – happy, worried, con - tented, scared, excited, sad, confused... You may need practice in getting in tune with your inner self.

Many start by writing their activities and expanding upon them. Thoughts, ideas and feelings start flowing freely after awhile. Questions and problems appear clearer once committed to paper. Like magic, solutions start revealing themselves to you. Ninety percent of the answer lies in the question. This process lets you constantly reframe your thinking and perceptions.

Eventually, you will enter a state of conscious and con - tinuous self-improvement with focus – a form of directed consciousness. Giving yourself permission to remove the distractions and noise of daily life adds clarity to your love life. Start your journal today. You'll be happy you did.

TIP.   Make a contract with yourself to do it for at least 21 days. Better yet, get two, one for yourself and the other for your lover. Then you can share your experiences during a quiet and intimate time together, if you choose.

SPECIAL OFFER: Get a journal you can carry with you all the time. *The Make Love With Life Journal,* AGES Publications, contains a quick tip ten point journal course, over 100 inspirational sayings and blank pages. Fits neatly in purses, briefcases, almost anything. Your investment is only $7.95. Tell them where you read this to get free ship - ping and handling! To order *The Make Love With Life Journal,* call toll free 1 800 263-1991.

Love begets love. This torment is my joy.

Theodore Roethke

The Law of Surrender

The secret of a stress free love life is found in the *Law of Surrender*. This is not about giving up, but going with the flow. Accepting reality in the way others perceive it will free you of the need to impose your reality on others. Giving up the need for control is truly liberating.

Many people choose to be like a fish swimming upstream – against the currents. The amount of energy expended is excessive. Better to follow the flow, and guide yourself accordingly. Then you use the power of the system and steer yourself in the direction most suitable for you.

In this way, your actions and thoughts can better be focused on your mission in life and those goals which rein - force it. Conserving your energy and being in partnership with the energy around you ends all struggle.

The *Law of Surrender* helps you live more fully in the moment.

Excerpt from *222 Ways to Make Love With Life: How to Love, Laugh & Live in the Moment*, by Ken Vegotsky, AGES Publications

Point to ponder

Someone once said, "Everything old is new again."

Just refer to ancient Chinese or Indian lovemaking manuals to find the truth in what they knew.

All love is sweet - given or returned.

Percy Shelley

Trivia of the most unusual lovemaking kind

Diminishing wildlife is a cause for concern, particularly with elephants since their population has been greatly diminished by ivory hunters. The elephant is on the verge of extinction. Attempts to help revitalize the population are being made.

Researchers in Africa decided to test a new system of delivering estrogen with a dash of testosterone to female elephants. They used large transdermal patches which delivered the sex hormones through the elephants skin.

The one year experiment was cut short because the female elephants were so randy they were exhausting the males. Twenty-five females were left on the patch, for a one year test period, to see what the affect is upon them.

Is that what they mean by the call of the wild? Who says sex is all in the head?

Vegetarians make better lovers!?

Vegetarianism enhances lovemaking. In meat eaters, the levels of the love hormone testosterone plummet almost 60 percent after a heavy meat meal. Lethargy can set in. Part of the reason is that the stomach uses more energy to process meats, fish and fowl than most vegetarian foods. The message here is eat lightly. Heat up or make low fat appetizers to consume as required to restore and prolong your energy levels if you're not already engrossed in the passion of the moment.

To love is to place our happiness in the happiness of another.

Gottfried von Leibniz

Alternative health lovemaking enhancer

The *nut of gold*, cola, is a marvelous fruit grown in Africa. Its stimulating properties have been known for thousands of years.

Used to overcome fatigue, it has long been prized for medicinal properties. African elders referred to it as the *makes them happy* fruit since it predisposed one to seek sexual pleasure.

Cola is so powerful it plays an important role in many pagan practices and rituals. In addition, Muslim religious leaders originally embraced its use since it made it easier to dispense with the con - sumption of alcohol. Today modern science has identified cola as having caffeine and theobromine which is an ingredient modern medicine uses for heart tonics. Of the two varieties white cola and red cola, the one most sought after is the red cola nut.

Excerpt from *For Lovers Only: 222 Romantic Hot Spots,*
AGES Publications

Love one another
but make not a bond of love.
Let it rather be a moving sea
between the shores of your souls.

Kahlil Gibran, *The Prophet*

Hot Tip — More Forbidden knowledge

Felling depressed, check out *St. Johns' Wort,* hypericum perforatum. In studies, this natural product was as effective as Prozac and many other anti-depressants without any of the side effects such as loss of sex drive.

Check out your health food store, naturopath or other complementary alternative health practitioner if you need help. If on anti-depressants, speak to your doctor first.

Well known trivia of the love offering kind

Love knows no bounds... The ruler of the Ottoman Empire, Suleiman the Magnificent, as a love offering gave the enslaved Roxelana her freedom, then married her. A citizen wrote, "This week there has occurred in this city an extraordinary event, absolutely unprecedented in the history of the Sultan's period. Suleiman has taken unto himself a slave woman from Russia as his empress."

Why is Valentine's Day a celebration?

The day was set aside to celebrate the feast day of the patron saint of love, Valentinus (St. Valentine). It has become a special day for engaged couples and anyone wishing to marry. The tra - dition was started by the Roman Catholic Church and is an ecumenical day celebrating love and affection.

Alternative health lovemaking enhancer

Ashwandha means *smells like a horse* and according to many it does! This Indian herb renews sexual vigor for some men.

Women should consider the dried leaf of a Mexican plant called *Daiana.* It renews or restores sexual vigor in many women.

Ginseng... an ancient Oriental tonic with benefits

It takes 4 to 6 weeks of regular use before the affects of ginsenosides, the active ingredients are felt. So plan ahead. The most potent ginsengs are

Chinese and Korean, next comes the Siberian and American ginsengs.

All ginseng labeled products are not necessarily effective. They may not have sufficient amounts or any of the active ingredients to be effective. Korean ginseng (Panax ginseng) is the most effec - tive for increasing sex drive in men. Check out your local health food store or pharmacy and get the brands that clearly label the amount of active ingredients. Read about this amazing plant – you'll be surprised at its many life enhancing benefits.

Bioforce, an A. Vogel company, produces one of the highest quality forms of this phytotherapeutic – medicinal plant based products in a liquid form. The liquid is called a tincture, which is in a diluted base of 91% alcohol, and has an incredibly long shelf-life. In many cases, govern - ment labeling laws impose an expiry date for natural prod - ucts. In some cases, this can be as short as three years for 100% natural products which actually have a shelf- life of 10, 15, or more years.

Interestingly, Kelpasan™ and Korean ginseng tinctures when combined have a synergistic effect – an effect greater than if taken separately – in stimulating low sex drive males. Kelpasan is derived from kelp and affects the thyroid. Care must be taken in many cases. For example, if you're allergic to iodine, on thyroid medica - tions, use lithium or have kidney problems, it is important that you consult a knowledgeable and qualified medical practitioner before using kelp based products.

Men and women prone to high blood pressure should not use Korean ginseng without a health pro - fessional's supervision.

> Nature is the medicine cabinet for making love with life - safely.

Plant based natural medicines are significantly safer than the vast majority of man made pharmacologically based products. When used wisely, they enhance the bodies natural abilities to heal and be healthy. Pharmacological products tend to mask symptoms without promoting the bodies wisdom to heal itself, and in many cases, create more and other problems. Numerous books and newsletters are available from proponents of such ideas such as Dr. Andrew Weil, Dr. Willix and others

Nature knows best. That's why most drugs are man made imitations of natural remedies.

Herbal pills are blends of ingredients that may increase your sexual appetite. Check out the health food stores for them. Many different formulations for men and women exist – Vive La Difference! According to many folks, they work.

To purchase natural products, a good source is Inside Bestsellers Product Information Services – toll free 1 800 595-1955.

Aromatherapy — Love, Lust and Cinnamon!?

Centuries ago, cinnamon was thought to be an aphrodisiac. Scientists have discovered that it stimulates the central nervous system. I mix a blend of 10 drops each of 100% pure botanical essential oils nutmeg and cinnamon to six ounces of water in a spray mister. They add a sensual mildly stimulating fragrance to the air. Two other essential oils that are sexually stimu - lating are sandalwood and ylang-ylang.

Numerous botanical based aromatherapy products are available in health food stores. Some you release in the air. Others you massage onto your partners body. Explore this avenue. You'll be delighted you did.

Loving way to share your fantasies and desires

Book marking is a wonderful way of gently expressing your sexual fantasies and desires. The way it works is simple.

Buy a book of erotic stories – or if you're a little skittish, borrow one from your library. The only problem is that you might feel pressured to return it. If you use the book, that's okay. Just be prepared to pay the fine... Hopefully, a big one.

Splurge. Buy a special book mark.

Find a fantasy story that particularly interests you... insert the book mark at that passage... leave the book on your partners night table or hand it to your partner to read at their leisure.

If your partner likes the idea expressed, the book with the bookmark in the same place is returned to you. The two of you reserve a time and... I'll leave the rest up to your imagination.

What does your partner do if the selection is not appealing? They read more stories... find one that appeals... insert the book mark to reveal their interest... leave it on your night table.

The main benefit is the gentle way of sharing those seldom discussed needs and wants that often create unnecessary stress – win-win negotiation for the bedroom. Worst is you become a very well read individual. Possibly very very well read!?

TIP: Joan Elizabeth Lloyd presents this idea, numerous erotic stories for lovers to share and helpful advice in her books, *Come Play With Me, If It Feels Good* and *Nice Couples Do,* published by Warner Books. A wonderful 180 minute audio cassette called *Nice Couples Do* from Time Warner Audiobooks combines parts of the three books in an abridged version. Missing a lot of the stories and detail, the tape is still a great place to start if you want to explore this aspect to Make Love and Make Love With Life.

Love is not getting, but giving.
    It is sacrifice. And sacrifice is glorious.

Joanna Field

Become a loving self-inviting guest chef

Invite yourself to a lovers home to make supper. I like to do Italian or Chinese Wok cooking and salads.

You bring the fixings and have them set the table. You can bring along candles, a potted flower or cut flowers for a center piece to create the mood. Make it an adventure in dining. Shared experiences build a bond of mutual respect and love.

TIP: Enhance the sense of adventure. Go shopping together to pick up the fixings for the meal . Try something new and unusual, such as star fruit, kiwi, sabra - prickly pear, it's prickly on the outside but deliciously sweet on the inside.

Hot cooking tip: If your making Italian, use angel hair pasta, also known as capellini pasta. It only takes two to three minutes to cook.

More of these quick, time saving and fun cooking tips will be available in *222 Ways for Quick & Fun Cooking: How to be a Gourmet Chef in Minutes – Mistakes Become Exotic Soups*. I'm having fun discovering and experimenting on these ideas now. If I can break myself away from eating long enough, I'll write the book. (If my waist is any indica - tion, there is a deliciously expanding market for fun and easy quick cooking ideas.)

In the meantime, until I get around to it, Brenda Ponichtera, a registered dietitian, has written two won - derful award winning cookbooks: *Quick & Healthy Recipes and Ideas*, as well as *Quick & Healthy, Volume 2*. ScaleDown Publishing, Inc. Available in bookstores or credit card orders call (514) 296-5859.

Hugs are a gentle form of healing massage
— love in disguise.

Trivia of the least important kind
How to Become a Prisoner of Love

A jailed burglar made an unauthorized arrangement with his girlfriend to have sex in her car. He arranged to work on an unescorted yard detail, before which they took a drive off the prison grounds and made love. When the girlfriend drove him back to the Metro West Detention Center, the guards nabbed the convict. His 20 minute tumble got an extra 30 days tacked onto his 90 day sentence.

That's how he became a prisoner of love. Any takers?

Aromatherapy is natures gift to humanity.

Basically there are four ways to use the essential oils from plants – orally, externally, nasal inhalation and in cooking.

Read a book by Valerie Woodward, Jo Serrentino or Tiessen. They are three top experts. You will discover how to use oils such as sandalwood, cinnamon and ylang-ylang, which may have aphrodisiac qualities.

An aromatherapy massage – external application combined with nasal titillation – is an incredible experi - ence that will really get you cooking.

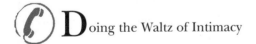

Doing the Waltz of Intimacy

The battle of the sexes is more about the differing styles of communications women and men have. If a man comes onto a woman, without invitation, he is seen as aggressive. If it is in response to subtle and sometimes not so subtle sig - nals from the woman, then it is more acceptable.

Recognizing the flirting signals a woman sends, puts a new perspective on the elegance of what I call the *Waltz of Intimacy*. More importantly once women are aware of these signaling techniques, they can better communicate their desires without fear of rejection. This assumes the man is aware of them as well. In both cases, these rituals of mating have evolved over centuries of socialization.

Each generation builds upon the foundation of the social skills of the prior one. Understandably, these signals reduce the pain of rejection. Still, they can create a lot of frustration. Personally, I prefer directness, yet that is not necessarily the way of the world.

Here are the top ten flirting signals women make according to relationship expert, Dr. Monica Moore:

1. Eyebrow flashing, an exaggerated raising of eyebrows, of both eyes, for a couple of seconds, followed by a rapid lowering to the normal position. Usually it's combined with a smile and eye contact.

2. The lip lick, wetting a lip or both lips.

3. Short darting glances, usually occurring in bouts with an average of three glances per bout.

4. The hair flip, she pushes her fingers through her hair.

5. Smiling coyly, sort of a half-smile showing little if any teeth in combination with a downward gaze or brief eye contact.

6. She bends over and whispers to a girlfriend.

7. Primping, patting or smoothing clothes even though there is no reason to.

8. Flashing a bit more leg, teasingly raises her skirt slightly.

9. She fondles keys, toys with stuff on the table or slides her hand up and down a glass.

10. She moves her body in a chair to the rhythm of music. This solitary dance is a gentle invitation to begin the *Waltz of Intimacy*. Go to it.

TIP: This is some of the fascinating information available in *Sex: A Man's Guide* by Stefan Betchel, Laurance Stains, and the editors of Men's Health books.

Ladies if you want to understand men better, then get a copy. You'll discover what men are being told about love and sex. Use it to gently communicate areas for growth with your male partner. Helping them is helping yourself.

Men, it's filled with pointers that can enhance your love making and intimacy abilities significantly. Being in a continuous state of self-improvement adds quality to your life and that of those around you.

Enrich your love life

Write yourself a love letter. Tell yourself about all your good qualities, and acts of kindness and love you have done and want to do. Plant the seeds of romance and watch them grow.

Seek wholeness in relationships.

That means you are starting out from a position of being and accepting who you are. Move away from the possession model which is a form of consumerism. Move toward that which is a way of celebrating each others uniqueness.

Enrich the life of your lover. Become a detective!?

Start checking out all the positive aspects of your partner. Now take love letter writing a step further. Like Star Trek, venture where no person has gone before. Write a love letter *about your partner* for yourself. List all the good points, loving acts or positive thoughts your partner shares with you. Here's how.

> Dear Friend/Partner,
> I am so lucky to know someone with all of the following good points, loving acts and thoughts you share with me.
> ...Then start listing and keep adding to the list.

Surprisingly, for some folks at first, focusing on another person's positive attributes is difficult. That's okay. We've been trained to sort negatively. This exercise is a way of learning to see the positive side. You are retraining yourself to find the good in others. It takes time. Take 21 days min-imum to create this life and love affirming list about your partner. Then once you've done it, surprise them with a letter acknowledging what you've brought into your con-scious awareness.

Point to ponder

What does *Psychology Today* have to say about love? The average person falls in love ten times before getting married.

Is that why they say practice makes perfect?

Trivia of the most important kind

Kissing is one of the most intimate sharings two human beings can have. Here are some tips for the lips.

Brush your teeth, tongue, gums – clean your mouth. Tease with your lips. Nibble. Tug. Pull... Gently alternate from soft to firm touching with the lips. Let your partner extend the invitation before frenching.

Practice. Practice. Practice. Like you did when you were teenagers. Savor the moments.

Be happy — use a squabble model

According to Larry Hof, M. Div., chief operating officer at the Marriage Council of Philadelphia, the key is to resolve more arguments. Men, here are steps you can take to have a better and healthier rela - tionship with your partner.

1. Let her vent. Move away from the idea of immedi - ately solving the problem. This allows her to get to the underlying issues, or what is the real problem.
2. Acknowledge and take her feelings seriously. An individual's feelings are not to be judged, but rather accepted.
3. Give up the need to be right or win a victory. Search for solutions.
4. Celebrate the resolution, whether that be going out for a treat, sharing a bowl of passion fruit or going for dinner.

Try these words… "I love you and I don't want this to stand between us." says Hof.

A complete re-evaluation takes place in your physical and mental being when you've laughed, loved and had some fun.

Catherine Ponder

Classic erotic grape treat.

Peel off the outer skin of the grape before eating. This removes a source of bitterness. The grapes taste so sweet!

Great if your alone, but even better when you share them with your partner — Listen to that mmmmmm.

(Seedless grapes are even less bitter.)

79

Sixty seconds to success in
Making Love With Life and your partner

Discover *The Flexible Affirmation*™ focusing technique
that creates positive outcomes in your life. Tap into
the magical loving powers of your mind today.

During the depths of my recovery from a near-fatal
accident, this gift from on high gave me hope to deal with
intense chronic pain. Drugs didn't work. Surgery lessened
it a bit. Every day the pain killed a little bit more of my
mind, body and spirit. I was desperate. Desperate enough
that I tried to take my own life.

The Flexible Affirmation is one of the tools I unleashed
while striving to survive and thrive in a world gone awry.
Use this technique now. Use it until your loving dreams,
goals or wishes come true. Frequent repetition to yourself
is important.

If you desire to change a specific behavior, commit to
saying it for at least 21 days. By the end of that time,
you'll be amazed at the success you have with it.
If you have a goal that takes a long time, then use
it daily and keep repeating it in your head until it comes to
pass. Here's an example.

> Am I attracting love into my life? Yes!
> When? Now!
> How? Through self-love and self-discipline!

Another example, on a slightly lighter side.

> Am I losing weight? Yes!
> When? Now!
> How? Through self-love and self-discipline!

Here's how it works. You ask yourself three questions.
The first one practices self forgiveness and imme -
diately puts a positive outcome in place of the
negative behavior or situation. It sets your mind's
eye and heart in a better direction. Saying **YES**, is
your internal commitment to a winning result.

The second question *'When?'* deals with making it happen in the present moment. It is the most critical step taking away thoughts of delaying – procrastination.

'How?' is the cherry on top of the cake. This third questions raises you above the idea that the outside world controls you and places the power of your thoughts and actions right back where they belong – inside you!

You've now set the direction and fueled your desires with self-empowerment in this moment. Isn't Making Love With Life discovering ways to live and love yourself in the moment! Yes!

> TIP: You can strengthen the affirmation by writing it on a small card. Carry it with you wherever you go. Post notes
> throughout your home and office with Flexible Affirmations and read them daily. I post them in the bathroom, kitchen, car, office, anywhere I use a space frequently.

Excerpt from *222 More Ways to Make Love With Life*,
Ken Vegotsky, AGES Publications

Trivia symbol of love

Herbalist Nicholas Culpeper wrote, "Venus owns this tree... the fruit provokes lust."

Arabs and Chinese regard this fruits deep fur-edged cleft as symbolic of female genitalia. The Chinese see the fruit's sweet juices as symbolic of the effluvia of the vagina. This fruit has been used almost universally to describe sexually appealing pretty women. What is it? Peaches.

> P.S. The English describe a house of prostitution as a "peach house." Is that why "Peachy keen" is such a popular phrase?

Only those who dare, truly live – truly love.

Ruth Freedman

Trivia of the sweetest kind

Chocolate may not be bad for you!? Scientists have discovered that chocolate may help release endorphins, thus creating a short lived, mildly euphoric state. In moderation, this may be beneficial to your wellbeing.

> ADVENTURE TIP: Certain chocolates have lower melting points or come in a spread. With a partner, melted or spread chocolate applied strategically and lovingly, can be quite an all consuming treat.

One *more* thing you can do to enrich your love life

Call up your lover and leave a romantic or inspirational saying on their answering machine if they don't answer. If they answer, tell them that you wanted to add a little sun - shine to their day with a saying.

Hey guys, you can do it. Take a saying from this book.

Life's sweetest joys are hidden in unsubstantial things;
an April rain, a fragrance, a vision of blue wings.

Mary Riley Smith

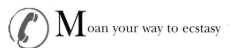 Moan your way to ecstasy

Communication during intimate moments is like a road map for you and your partner. The problem is that words just don't seem to cut it in the throes of passion.

Heighten your pleasure by using moans and groans. Increasing or decreasing their intensity is another way to express your desires, needs and wants.

Show them with sound what pleasures you. It is an

acceptable way to indicate what you want. Discover and explore your partners pleasure points. Let your partner dis - cover the magic of hitting your hot spots right on.

Surprisingly these can change from one loving experience to the next. Moans and groans add chemistry to the moment. Sounds become aphrodisiacs for increased sexual tension.

Mmmmmmm... sounds good to me. Does it to you?

No sex please — just massage

Blow your mind. Honor your partner. Make love in the middle of the night. Discover the sensuality without the sexuality. One partner gently massages the other into a state of arousal. NO sex please – just massage. Don't touch the genitals.

Savor the journey...

Lose yourself in the moment

Dance freely and wildly. Play wild music. Put on comfortable clothing (optional). Throw your arms and hands out. Let your cares and worries fly away. Spin, twirl and become one with the music and the song in your heart.

This can be done alone or with others. Do it with a lover and feel the energy.

Many mystical systems use this as a way of reaching ecstasy! At weddings, dancing is the part all share in tribute to the couple – trying to get the ecstasy ball rolling, so to speak.

Great examples of the power of losing one's self in dance are the sequences in these classic movies *Zorba the Greek* and *Fiddler on The Roof*. Rent the videos and see for yourself.

Well known trivia of the love offering kind

The Hanging Gardens of Babylon in Iraq were one of the seven wonders of the ancient world. Fact is, they were not hanging gardens, but gardens on terraces or balconies.

When King Nebuchadnezzar brought his new wife from Medes, she missed the lush growth and mountains of her homeland. In 600 B.C., he started building his gift of love. It was a 400 foot high square building, having five terraces, each densely planted with flowers, grass and fruit trees. Slaves and oxen manned pumps below to irrigate the vegetation. Amid the gardens and artificial rain, his queen held court.

Natural lovemaking enhancer... Zinc!?

For centuries, oysters have been reputed to be an aphrodisiac. According to Sheldon Hendler, M.D., Ph.D., of the University of California in San Diego, oysters are high in a mineral component important to the prostate and semen – zinc. Men who are experiencing a reduced sex drive and low sperm count may be suffering from a severe to moderate zinc deficiency. If so, they may benefit from oysters and other foods which are rich in zinc such as wheat germ, whole-grain products, lean meat and seafood.

Not an Aphrodisiac

Alcohol can dull sensations rather than enhance lovemaking. In minimal to moderate amounts, it may reduce inhibitions enough to enhance the experience. Don't drink and drive may be applied to sex in that the disadvantages may out weigh the benefits.

Treat yourself and your lover to a massage

There are numerous kinds of massages. My favorite kind is called Swedish massage. Combine that with the healing or stimulating properties of an aromatherapy essential oil in a good base carrier oil and you'll feel like you're in heaven.

> TIP: Budget tight, then call a local school where masseuses are trained. They need to practice on people. Volunteer – you'll be glad you did!
> Health food stores, department stores and The Body Shop may have premixed aromatherapy massage oils.

Secret for life long happiness

When you do something for someone else,
do it out of love — expect nothing in return.

Candle light – a great way to be in the moment

Throw in a dash of your favorite music, a pinch of incense and dim the lights. Now, slowly breath in and savor the ambience. Alone, time stands still... Shared with a lover, it flies by.

Grunt and groan lovemaking enhancer

Exercise is an aphrodisiac as well as being great for physical and mental health. Numerous studies indicate the benefits from exercising – reduces incidence of coronary heart disease, improves sexual functioning, enhances mood, helps with weight loss... and the list gets longer and longer.

Aerobic exercise, where you increase your hearts ability to function, can create a natural high through the release of endorphins. During exercise, some enthusiasts trigger the body's own antidepressant and pain relief mechanisms, and produce endogenous opiates or natural morphine. Surprisingly, those who were the most sedentary got the most initial benefit.

In women who exercised at least 3.5 hours a week, Swedish researchers discovered that exercise helped reduced or eliminate hot flashes during menopause. Exercise was also reported to reduce the effects of osteo - porosis, increase muscle mass – meaning you slim down even though you may weigh the same, instill a greater sense of freedom and improve the ability to enjoy one's feminine sexual side. The idea of use it or lose it is now being scien - tifically proven.

> TIP: Don't call it exercise. That sounds too much like work. Turn recreational activities, such as going for a walk, into opportunities to help your body and connect with a partner. Removing distractions and spending quiet time with another increases intimacy and connection. Add a dash of hand holding and occasional stops for gentle back or neck massages and you're growing the most powerful aphrodisiac, love.

Back to school

Take or share an adult conscious raising course on relationships, loving, how to strip for your lover, how to catch a mate, flirting… There are public seminar centers throughout the USA and Canada. You can meet some of the greatest educators and writers of our time at these courses. Here is a partial list of such groups. Look the numbers up in your phone book or check out your local health food store for a free course catalog.

The Learning Annex: San Diego, CA; Los Angeles, CA;
   San Francisco, CA; New York, NY; Washington, D.C.;
   Toronto ON, Canada
The Learning Connection: Providence, RI
The Learning Exchange: Sacramento, CA;
   Wethersfield, CT
Learning Tree University: Chatworth, CA
Leisure Learning Unlimited: Houston, TX
Oasis: Chicago, IL
Discover U: Seattle, WA
Colorado Free U: Denver, CO
Open U: Minneapolis, MN
Knowledge Shop: Orlando, FL
Baywinds: Tampa, FL

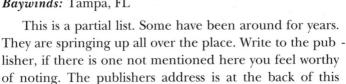

This is a partial list. Some have been around for years. They are springing up all over the place. Write to the pub - lisher, if there is one not mentioned here you feel worthy of noting. The publishers address is at the back of this book.

If you take a course I'm giving, feel free to come up and share an Hawaiian Hug with me. They are great!

All things are difficult before they are easy.

John Norley

Romantic and erotic music for your ears

You and your lover record the sounds of love - making. Have fun. Do it as a fantasy that you both share. Create an evolving dialogue of romantic sensual love - making. Make a copy so each of you have one to awaken your inner self. Use before a romantic evening together, if separated for a long time, in the car – only if your parked.

> TIP: Too embarrassed to do it, then take a peak at the back
>   of this book for the audio tape version of *Je T'aime* (I
>   Love You).

Eight keys for achieving a happier love life

1) Be flexible. There is no single approach that works for everyone.

2) Many possible solutions exit for any situation.

3) The problem and solution may not be related.

4) The best approach is usually the simplest and least invasive.

5) People can and do get better quickly.

6) Change happens constantly.

7) Focus on your resources and strengths, not your weaknesses and deficits.

8) Let go of the past by focusing on the future.

Focus on these three aspects – solutions, changing your attitudes and positive actions leading to positive outcomes. This is the core of Rational-Emotive Therapy and the main subject of numerous books that say *to feel good, think positive and do positive.*

Point to ponder today

Life is a celebration. Love Living. Live Loving.

Alternative health love enhancer

Making love with life requires an energy boost at times. Here are five ways to boost your energy levels.

1. I use two essential oils for this - peppermint and lemon to quickly invigorate me. I put a drop on a handker - chief/face cloth and inhale their essence. Lemon boosts my feelings of wellness. The Japanese use it in their office air conditioning systems. It reduced data clerk entry errors by a whopping 54%.

2. Invest in an air purifier.

   TIP: I have dozens of the best and cheapest air purifiers on the face of the earth spread throughout my home – plants. Bionaire Corporation of Allendale, New Jersey produces an excellent HEPA grade, hospital clean air quality stan- dard, home air cleaner. Their toll free consumer informa- tion numbers are: U.S.A. 1 800 253-2764, Canada 1 800 561-6478.

3. Vitamin deficiencies are a common cause of fatigue. I use a B-complex supplement along with iron and magnesium supplements when necessary. The B vitamins are water soluble and should be replen- ished daily. Water soluble means that your body distrib- utes the nutrient through liquids, like blood. Excess amounts are removed through urination and sweat. The iron is particularly beneficial to women, since men- struation causes iron depletion in the body. Good sources of iron are bananas, apricots, sea vegetables, beans and whole-rye grain.

4. Lack of good quality rest and sleep suck the energy from you. Drinking chamomile tea, or other specially formulated herbal teas, helps me and my children sleep better.

5. And finally, let there be light. Expose yourself to at least 15 minutes of sunlight a day. Our bodies produce vitamin D this way. If indoors, you may want to use full spectrum lighting. You'll be amazed at the difference in the quality of light. Health food stores and places like The Home Depot carry these types of lighting.

T ry these for a better love life

Seek to know yourself and accept others.
Reconciliation. Reconciliation. Reconciliation.
Lessons from ancient mystics of the East.

Get a natural buzz… a natural hot flash

Niacin, a vitamin from the B family, can create a feeling of being flushed. It takes about 20 to 30 minutes before it is felt. Oh what a flush it is!

Extreme caution is urged since improper use can have harmful affects upon your system.

Alternative health love enhancer

DHEA boosts your sex drive, according to Dr. Ray Sahelian, author of *DHEA: A Practical Guide,* Avery Publishing Group. It is a hormone made by the adrenal glands that appears to boost libido – sex drive, enhance mood, increase energy levels, improve the immune system and a host of other possibilities. Most of the evidence is allegorical or from animal based research at this time.

CAUTION: A friend of mine was scheduled for an angioplasty – heart operation. He decided to first try chela - tion therapy, a technique used to remove heavy metals from the blood. His health practitioner used DHEA as part of the treatment. After months of chelation therapy, my friend canceled his surgery. Today, he looks great and says he feels better than he has in years.

P.S. He's in his 60's and recently married.

Research into the benefits of DHEA is in its infancy. Speak to your Doctor before using this hormone for any reason, even to boost your sex drive.

Natural lovemaking enhancer

Asparagus!? Folklore has seen its shape as a sign of sexual enrichment. Asparagus is rich in potas - sium, calcium and phosphorus which are needed for maintenance of a high energy level. It contains a diuretic that increases the amount of excreted urine and excites the urinary passages. However, another component of asparagus, aspartic acid, neutralizes excess amounts of ammonia in the body. Ammonia may cause sexual disinterest and apathy.

It's healthy, low fat and nutrient rich. I steam asparagus for a few minutes until it becomes a vibrant green, then eat it plain or sometimes with a dip. Most often I throw it into rice and noodle recipes I am creating. I guess you can have your asparagus and eat it too.

Natures lovemaking enhancer

Menopause ...an aphrodisiac!? ...for men!? ...for women!? ...a time for celebration? ...a rite of passage and inner evolution? Menopause is an aphrodisiac with a twist. Men, as well as women, have a change of life.

In men, this tends to lead to a decrease in their sexual drive and the urgency to fulfill their masculinity through physical conquest. They can still impregnate women and they still have the responsibility to take precautions. More importantly, they can now savor the journey, as much as the act, no longer guided solely by the testosterone imperative. In essence, men no longer think with a six inch brain as they did through most of their prior adulthood. This is when their partner can seize the opportunity to help them become gentler and better lovers.

Women are freed from the fears of pregnancy and the attendant need for birth control methods. Increased amounts of testosterone (androgens) in women combined with a more relaxed attitude about their sexuality leads to a much more satisfying love life.

Menopause is a time of transition where the body, mind and soul appear to attain a more integrated and level state of being.

Be embraced. Share this neat little poem with a lover and throw in a hug, of course.

Hugs...

It's wondrous what a hug can do
A hug can cheer you when your blue
A hug can say "I love you so" or
"Gee, I hate to see you go."
A hug is "welcome back again" and
"Great to see you!" "Where have you been?"
A hug can soothe a small child's pain
And bring a rainbow after rain.
The Hug! There's no doubt about it
We scarcely could survive without it.
A hug delights and warms and charms
It must be why "God" gave us arms.
Hugs are great for fathers and mothers.
Sweet for sisters, swell for brothers
And chances are your favorite aunts
Love them more than potted plants.
Kittens crave them: puppies love them
Heads of state are not above them.
A hug can break the language barrier
And make travels so much merrier.
No need to fret above your store of 'em
The more you give, the more there's of 'em.
So stretch those arms without delay
And give someone a hug today.

Author Unknown

Alternative health love enhancer

Ho shou wu is used by herbalists to boost sperm production in men and general fertility in women. It also appears to nourish hair and teeth.

92

Natural lovemaking enhancer

Lobster has been described by many writers as a love food with aphrodisiac properties.

The myth of Aphrodite, the goddess of love born from sea foam, is the basis of this one since the sea supposedly shares Aphrodite's power.

The Tantra of lovemaking and romance

This Far Eastern Indian system encourages prolonged lovemaking, but less stress is placed on a man's ability to hold back his orgasm.

Some of the things you'll discover include: deep breathing techniques, locking eyes to intensify the sensual and sexual connections, Tantric kissing where he inhales while she exhales and vice versa... plus much more to extend and increase orgasmic pleasure.

Lovers mirror the divine union as they share the most sacred of acts, connecting directly with the life force. You'll discover the erotic arts and the meditative traditions that empower you both. You'll transcend time and space, reaching a state of blissful partnership with your partner and the universe.

Tip: *The Art of Sexual Magic*, by Margo Anand is a wonderful book. Better yet, Sounds True Audio of Boulder, Colorado created a fantastic audio cassette program, you can savor and enjoy. The price is well worth it. The journey is delightful. To order it in North America call toll free 1 800 333-9185, Overseas call (303) 449-6229 or fax (303) 665-5292. Ask for their catalog of audio and video products. It's super!

P.S. I'm not on commission, nor am I related to any of the folks at Sounds True, nor the author who brought this light into our lives. When I find something that can help you save money and time and better make love with life, I share it.

Aromatherapy — aphrodisiac massage oil blend

A massage oil blend, which uses essential botanical oils, can easily be mixed at home. Aromatherapy massage enhances sensuality and excitement by raising awareness through touch, smell and sight. A good starting place is with this mixture.

In an an oil base of safflower and almond oil (5 1/2 ounces or 150 ml) mix these essential oils: ylang-ylang (15 drops), sandalwood (15 drops), frankincense (10 drops) and bay (5 drops).

It is okay to vary it slightly if you find a formula better suited to you and your partner. Create a deliciously sensual massage moment in your life. Be creative and have fun.

> Tip.   A source for quality aromatherapy and natural products is
> Inside Bestsellers Product Information Services – call toll
> free 1 800 595-1955.

Lord, make me an instrument of thy peace.
   Where there is hatred... let me sow love.
   Where there is injury... pardon.
   Where there is doubt... faith.
   Where there is despair... hope.
   Where there is darkness... light.
   Where there is sadness... joy.

O Divine Master, grant that I may not so much seek
   To be consoled... as to console.
   To be understood... as to understand.
   To be loved... as to love.

Saint Francis of Assisi

The symphony of life is best heard in the silence between the notes. In fact, in a real symphony, it is the silences which make the music work best. It is during those silences that lovers share in all their glory.

Expressions of the love offering kind

Diamonds are a girls best friend!?
What if it is the size of a baseball?
Richard Burton spent $1,050,000 to buy a 69.42 carat diamond from Cartier for Elizabeth Taylor. Other baubles he bought for Elizabeth include the 33.9 carat Krupp diamond ($350,000), the Ping-Pong diamond ($38,000), La Peregrina pearl ($37,000), an emerald ($93,000), a $65,000 sapphire brooch and at $125,000 the most expensive mink coat in the world. Those prices were when a buck was worth a buck. Now that's what I call a big spender! They got married in Montreal, Quebec, Canada.

Well known trivia of the love offering kind
A Gift of Love – the Taj Mahal!!!

Upon the death of his favorite wife, Mumtaz Mahal, the grief stricken emperor of the Moguls, Shah Jahan ordered the building of the white alabaster mau - soleum. She died giving birth to her 14th child in 1631. It took 15 years for twenty thousand workmen to build the beautiful costly tomb. The Taj Mahal stands on the Jumna River in India. Inside, a reflecting pool and marble pavement surround a walled garden.

Discover the exotic splendor and beauty of the land where the Kama Sutra was written, the home of the Taj Mahal.

Excerpt from *For Lovers Only: 222 Romantic Hot Spots*,
Ken Vegotsky, AGES Publications

Surrender…

to the greatest power in the universe – love.
The universe will rejoice.

Trivia of the most lovemaking kind
that pays dividends!?!

According to *Psychology Today,* "Women who read romance novels make love 74% more often than woman who do not read romance novels."

Ladies, LionHearted Publications has great romance novels which are not available in bookstores. They range from historical to modern settings. The three I reviewed were great reads.

An interesting twist is that LionHearted empowers their writers by giving them a better, bigger and faster return for their labors. Empowering writers and readers is their mis - sion.

Tip: Statistics indicate that 5% of men covertly read romance novels. The owners of LionHearted Publications believe it is now 10% and increasing. Ladies, lend the guys your romance novels. You'll add zing to your love life if you tell them that men who read them benefit from the knowl - edge. Guys, what a wonderful gift these would make for your partners.

Hot tip: They are located in Zephyr Cove, Nevada. In the USA and Canada to order call their toll free number 1 888 lion-hrt (546-6478) Overseas orders call (702) 588-1388. Ask for their super special book package offer and how you can make money sharing the LionHearted Romance novel series. Tell them Ken Vegotsky, the author of the Make Love With Life books, sent you.

Trivia of the most important kind — great reason for getting men to commit to a relationship

Dr. Linda Waite of the University of Chicago says married men have lower rates of alcohol and drug abuse, and depression than single men. In addition, they are financially better off and their sex lives are generally better than before marriage.

John Gottman, a University of Washington psychologist

in an interview in *USA Today* said, "...substantial benefits evidence that marriage disproportionately benefits men..."

in regards to how happy and healthy they are.

In closing, a Canadian health study in Ontario reported that a 50 year old married man is expected to live 3.7 years longer than his bachelor counterpart.

> Get married.
> Live long
> and prosper!

Wow! If those aren't great reasons to get married guys, you better have your head examined. Sorry guys... I call it like I see it.

Love trivia of the mind expanding kind

According to a survey which rated lovemaking sexual experiences, 24% of the adult population said the closest that they have come to a spiritual experience is during orgasm.

What makes this fascinating is that the French describe the orgasm as **Le petit mort** which means *The little death.*

Unusual love trivia of the most important kind

According to Los Angeles sex researcher and therapist Marilyn Fithian, Ph.D., many women have orgasms and do not realize it.

She measured women's arousal by monitoring physical signs to determine if they orgasmed.

Measurements included lubrication and blood flow in the genitalia, heart rate going from 70 to 120 beats a minute, pupils expanding, changes to skins electrical con - ductivity, contractions to the pelvis, anus, vagina and uterus... plus other factors.

Volunteers were hooked up to monitors and asked to pleasure themselves. Their orgasms were recorded by the equipment. When asked if they had an orgasm, 75% of the women who had, said no.

Using biofeedback techniques, the women were taught to become aware of their orgasms. This was done by showing them when the physical measurements occurred on paper and training them to identify their orgasms.

T rivia of the most important kind

Researchers say that a sneeze has the same force and effect upon the human body as an orgasm.

> P.S.　I don't know about you, but I'd be willing to sign up for a seminar on *Sneezing Yourself Into Ecstasy.*

V ery risque fantasy follies

The *Story of O* is an adult fiction written anonymously in the middle of the twentieth century and first published in France. It is a sadomasochistic fable along the lines of the writings of the Marquis De Sade.

Reviewers say it transcends the pornographic and even erotic. It is a story about a beautiful fashion photographer and her lover. She descends into a world of subjugation motivated by the desire to please her lover.

The critically acclaimed 1973 movie *Last Tango in Paris* is loosely based on the *Story of O*. It stared Marlon Brando in one of his best performances and Maria Schneider in a critically acclaimed role. It is considered to be one of director Bernado Bertollucci's most provocative films. Definitely, not for children. The book and movie are for adults wishing to explore their fantasies in this fashion. Both are con - sidered to be top rated modern adult fantasy classics.

Unique expressions of the love offering kind

How about an island as a wedding gift? Aristotle Onassis gave Jackie Kennedy a share of the island of Skorpios when they got married in 1968 and a gem wardrobe estimated to cost $1.2 million. That was only for starters. Some say he lavished $20 million of plea - sures upon her during their first year of married life.

Now that's what I call getting a charge out of life and love.

Ponder this

Why is it that
the little things in life count the most.

Connecting to a source that prevents many lovers from being fully in the moment with their lovers

Self-awareness can mean connecting to your inner child and the parental or societal rules imposed upon you. Guilt and shame are just two manifes - tations that prevent you from living, loving and being fully in the moment with your lover.

This idea helps release you from many of the ties that bind you, holding you back from being all you can be.

Reflect on your actions today. Did you blame someone? Did you say I want more and I want it now? Did you yell needlessly to be heard?

Where did you learn these tactics for survival? The dif - ference between survival and thriving is learning to take self-responsibility.

Learning to become self-aware of your emotions, and recognizing when and why you're experiencing them, is very helpful and liberating.

Discover the desserts of your labors
   Lovemaking Afterplay

Had a wild passionate evening of lovemaking? Okay 15 minutes. Now all he wants to do is roll over and fall asleep. All you want is to be hugged, cuddled and shared with? Seductively suggest afterplay to him. Here are keys to making it work.

1. Don't analyze your experience, share your feelings and intimate thoughts.
2. Don't bring the past into bed with you.
3. Caress and cuddle for at least 8-10 minutes... or longer.
4. Say, "I love you," with meaning.

Love is mushrooming... a natural sex enhancer

Aphrodisiac fungi power – truffles! Also con - sidered one of the ultimate food experiences. They are similar to oysters in that this expensive underground fungus is mainly water and rich in protein.

An old French proverb warns that *"those who wish to lead a virtuous life should abstain from truffles."* Guess many didn't listen to the proverb. Here are some of the notable ones: Casanova, Marquis de Sade, Rabelais, Napoleon and Madame Pompadour. They lavished high praise on the aphrodisiac powers of this lowly fungus.

Treasure the love you receive above all.
   It will survive
long after your gold and good health have vanished.

Og Mandino

Enrich your lover's life

Send a love note to your lover — just like that.

Love is like a seed... plant it and watch it grow

Positive self-talks, also known as affirmations, are recordings you can choose to play in your mind. Using them will enhance your love life. Repeat this one to yourself through out the day.

I love myself.

Anniversary celebrations with a twist

Getting older beats the alternative. Aging is something to be celebrated. Here's a unique approach. Rather than getting gifts, give them to those you love. Being thankful is one of the simplest ways to acknowledge all life has to offer.

Next time it is your birthday, anniversary or any celebration, give everyone you invite a small gift or token of your appreciation. The difference between gifts of obligation and gifts of love is quite large.

A timeless gift of love

The Original Time Capsule Company of Greenfield, Indiana, created the *New Baby's Time Capsule* and *Our Wedding Time Capsule*. Beautifully crafted canisters, loaded with wonderful materials and ideas, can help you remember those cherished moments in your life. To find out where you can get your time capsule in North America call their toll free number 1 800 729-8463, overseas call (317) 891-8463. Create your own with your partner.

Acupressure or reflexology for the hurried person

Take a tennis ball and roll it under your bare feet. Did you enjoy it? Yes! Then explore the healing power of a reflexology session with a trained specialist or a close friend who will rub your feet. …Aaahhh!

Enjoying all life has to offer requires that your body and mind function at their best. Tapping into ways that help you function better, so that you can better make love with life, is very important.

Vitality, youthfulness, energy and clear thinking are greatly enhanced with proper nutrition. Unfortunately, the farming and food processing techniques of the last fifty years have created foods with reduced or depleted nutri - tional value. Also, the increased use of fertilizers, pesti - cides, preservatives… has increased our exposure to toxic chemicals. So many of our foods, considered to be health giving or healing, no longer have sufficient nutrients for our body's optimal functioning. This subtly affects your love of life and your love life.

Many of us recognize this and look for nutritional sup - plements. Then we find ourselves faced with enormous amounts of information and misinformation that make it difficult to determine the best forms of supplementation.

Two critical points are how much of it actually gets used by your body, and how quickly it gets to where it has to go in your body. The delivery system, how it's administered, determines the absorption rate and amount of a supplement that is actually available for use by your body. The label may say one thing, but reality says only what the body can and does use is effective. Use the following chart the next time you go to buy supplements.

According to the
Physicians Desk Reference #49,
this is what they say about supplements:

Tablets – regular	drink and swallow, 2 to 4 hours for absorption. Your body absorbs 5-10% of the nutrients.
Gel caps –	drink and swallow, 1 to 3 hours for absorption. Your body absorbs 15-20% of the nutrients.
Chelated – Pills	drink and swallow, 4 to 6 hours for absorption. Your body absorbs 25-30% of the nutrients.
Patches –	apply to skin, 3 to 5 hours for absorption. Your body only gets to use 45-50% of the nutrients.
Liquids –	sublingual through the mouth, 30 minutes for absorption. Your body absorbs 60-70% of the nutrients.
Injections –	intramuscular injections through the skin. Ten minutes for absorption. Your body absorbs 70-80% of the nutrients.
Liposome – oral sprays	through the mouth - 30 seconds for absorption. Your body absorbs 90% of the nutrients.

Spray-ceuticals™ which are from a company called TOTALlink, have revolutionized the vitamin, mineral, enzyme and hormone supplementation business with their line of products. I've tried them and found them easy to use and carry, great tasting and comparatively cost effective. They contain no preservatives no additives and have a 2 year shelf life.

> The medicine cabinet for life surrounds us – mother nature makes love with life and energizes us.

To get information about their products and other alternative and natural health products call Inside Bestseller Product Information Services and ask for the TOTALlink information pack of literature plus audio tape by Dr. Regelson M.D. The cost is $10. Their toll free number is 1 800 595-1955, Overseas call (519) 396-9553 or fax (519) 396-9554.

P.S. When you call Inside Bestseller Product Information Services, ask them to also send you information about YU-CCAN herbal drink products. I use their excellent herbal tonics to help my body maintain and energize itself. I suf - fered a lot of body damage from an accident. According to the manufacturer, the product is so superior and of such high quality that it is one of the few herbal products the government of China imports for its therapeutic value.

Try this for a love life boost...

Pretend you're dating again. Go to a lounge or bar you've never been to. Check out a fancy hotel nearby. Have your significant other come onto you as if you've never met. How? You sit at the table and they send you a drink. After it's delivered, you casually stroll over and continue the flirtation…

P.S. Surprise your lover by reserving a room ahead of time. Make arrangements for the kids so you don't have to rush home. Pack for two and plan for an evening of renewed romance.

Super secret for building a loving relationship

An easy way to discover how to love another is to watch how they love. If they mainly express their love with words, then use words. If they mainly express their love using touch, do the same. If they mainly express their love with visual signs, then use visual signs.

Each of us is unique in our styles of sharing. These are three of the many ways people express themselves. Tune into the method of communication your lover uses the most, then mirror it.

The first challenge is to discover how you prefer to express love most of the time. Start now and share the knowledge with our lover.

Discover a world of hot, erotic romance between the covers – the covers of a book by one of the twentieth century's great steamy writers. What did you think I meant?

The classic works of D. H. Lawrence, *Lady Chatterley's Lover* and *Women in Love,* will steam up your imagination. Take a peak between the covers and let your body use its own wisdom to get cooking.

> Trivia: *John Thomas and Lady Jane* was the original title of *Lady Chatterley's Lover.*

Discover... the Law of Detachment

Powerful... Simple... Effective... This idea helps you deal with any negative vibrations affecting your sense of serenity and peaceful coexistence with the universe.

These are the four D's to apply when dealing with life problems such as criticism, divorce, someone else's anger or anytime negative vibrations are affecting your sense of serenity and peaceful coexistence.

Detach yourself from events.

Decide to focus on love or positive outcomes.

Divide assets – treat inanimate things as just that, treat them as objects.

Deal with your own stuff.

This is how Joyce, an attendee at my seminar at the Celebration Center of Religious Science in Fall Church, Virginia, summarized the idea that I shared with them called Divorce, the Healing Relationship.

Mind expanding tip

 Give the man in your life a Harlequin or Silhouette novel. It may help him better appreciate and accept your ideas of romance.

If he needs some encouragement to read it, just tell him you'll give a brief quiz, and if he passes, then you'll… I'll leave that up to your imagination.

Men, give the woman in your life a copy of this book. (Okay I admit it. I'm an unabashed believer in what I write about.)

Show her you care.

One more thing you can do to enrich your life

Listen actively to what your lover is saying.

Discover the magic

New Women magazine reports the main ingredient to a happy relationship is support. If couples support each other's goals and dreams 100% not only does this enhance the overall relationship, it boosts each partner's chances of successfully reaching their goals.

Live your life each day as you would climb a mountain.

An occasional glance toward the summit keeps the goal in mind, but many beautiful scenes are to be observed from each new vantage point. Climb slowly, steadily, enjoying each passing moment; and the view from the summit will serve as a fitting climax for the journey.

H. Melcher

Unique expressions of the love offering kind

The Gift of the Magi is O. Henry's famous Christmas story. It shares the personal sacrifices that two young lovers made for each other at Christmas time. Jim sold his family heirloom, a pre-cious gold watch, to buy Della, his wife, an expensive tortoiseshell comb. She cut off her beautiful long hair to buy Jim, her husband, a platinum watch-fob chain.

There is beauty in the forest
    when the trees are green and fair.
There is beauty in the meadow
    when wild flowers scent the air.
There is beauty in the sunlight
    and the soft blue beams above.
Oh, the world is full of beauty
    when the heart is full of love.

Author Unknown

Last point to ponder

Savor the magic of this simple blend for living, laughing and loving in the moment. Playfully share the ingredients. Remember, *gently stirred – not shaken.* Add a *dash* — a big heaping *dash* — of sharing the fun with a partner today!

See You In the Next Book

To Write To The Authors

Dear Reader, Meeting Planner, or Speakers' Bureau

Both authors and the publisher appreciate hearing from you and learning of the benefits and enjoyment you received from this book. We cannot guarantee that every letter written can be answered by the authors, but all will be forwarded. To help ensure that your letter is answered, or to arrange a speaking engagement or seminar, please write to the appro - priate address below.

Make your convention or meeting a memorable experi - ence. Book Ken Vegotsky as your Keynote Speaker or sem - inar/workshop facilitator. He is an entertaining educator. A good time is guaranteed for all!

Ken says, "May I always give you more than you pay for. May you always want to pay me more."

That is Ken's philosophy and a fact!

In the U.S.A.

Madame E or Ken Vegotsky
c/o AGES Publications™
8391 Beverly Blvd., #323-ML
Los Angeles, CA 90048
Please enclose a self-addressed, stamped envelop for reply,
and $3.00 to cover costs.

In Canada

Madame E or Ken Vegotsky
c/o AGES Publications™
1054-2 Centre St., #153-ML
Thornhill, Ontario, Canada L4J 8E5.
Please enclose a self-addressed, stamped envelop for reply,
and $4.00 to cover costs.

If outside the U.S.A. or Canada

Enclose international postal reply coupon with a
self-addressed envelope and $3.00 U.S. to cover costs.

Contact Coordinator – phone (519) 396-9553 – fax (519) 396-9554

*A Great Gift for the
Special People In Your Life!*

The Ultimate Power
A National Bestseller!

ISBN 1-886508-15-1

The Way You Look at Life
— and Death —
Will Never Be The Same

Take Control of Your Life
Become the Master of Your Destiny
Learn the Secrets of Living on Your Own Terms
Utilize Your Mind-Body-Soul Potential to
Gain Complete Happiness

"Wow – what a great book. If you are ready to turn on your Ultimate Power, read Ken's brilliant and illuminating book."

Mark Victor Hansen
co-author of Chicken Soup for the Soul
New York Times #1 Bestseller

"As a psychologist – and a human being – I recommend The Ultimate Power to people who suffer chronic pain as well as to people who are searching for their authentic voice and a new beginning to life."

Dr. J. Siegel, Psychologist

"Ken Vegotsky has written a GREAT book. A heroic book. He is the Victor Frankl of our day. You will want to pur - chase many copies to give to those you love, those who are discouraged, those who need to rise again from adversity."

Dottie Walters, President
Walters International Speakers Bureau
Author of Speak & Grow Rich

Stress Free Living
222 Ways to Live Stress Free

222 Ways to
Make Love With Life
How To
Love, Laugh &
Live in the Moment

Lessons from a
Near-Death
Experience
THE
ULTIMATE
POWER
HOW TO UNLOCK YOUR
MIND-BODY-SOUL POTENTIAL
Ken Vegotsky

222
More Ways
to
Make Love
With Life
More Ways for

FOR
LOVERS ONLY
222 Ways to
Enhance the Magic

The
Make Love
With Life
Journal

Ken Vegotsky
author of
The Ultimate Power
222 Ways to Make Love With Life
222 More Ways to Make Love With Life
FOR LOVERS ONLY

From AGES Publications

Books

+

Audio Tapes

The Ultimate Power
An eight cassette audio tape program. Includes the book. For you, a friend or a study group.

Hypnotic Journey of Gentle Surrender
A combination of guided imagery, breathing & relaxation techniques, and music.

The Gift of Laughter
The laughter of children mingled with the music of a babbling brook. Just plain old fun, helping to rekindle the child within.

Je T'aime (I Love You)
Sensual sounds of lovers and nature.

Order Form

BOOKS	Qty	Price	Total
The Make Love With Life Journal over 100 inspirational & motivational sayings		$7.95	
222 Ways to Make Love With Life How To Love, Laugh and Live in the Moment		$7.95	
222 More Ways to Make Love With Life More Ways for Loving… Living in the Moment		$7.95	
For Lovers Only 222 Ways to Enhance the Magic		$7.95	
Stress Free Living – 222 Ways to Live Stress Free & Make Love With Life		$7.95	
The Ultimate Power How to Unlock Your Mind Body Soul Potential		$14.95	
AUDIO TAPES			
The Ultimate Power – 8 cassettes program includes the book		$89.95	
Hypnotic Journey of Gentle Surrender – Relaxation techniques		$9.95	
The Gift of Laughter helping to rekindle the child within		$9.95	
Je T'aime (I Love You) sensual sounds of lovers and nature		$9.95	
Sub-total			
(over $36 free delivery or $3.00 for 1st item + $0.50 for each additional item)　Shipping			
Total			

Name_____

Address _____

City _____ZIP _____

Phone _____

Please make certified check/money order payable to and send to
Adi, Gaia, Esalen Publications Inc.
8391 Beverly St. #323-ML, Los Angeles, CA 90048

VISA ❑   MasterCard ❑   American Express ❑
Call Toll free 1 800 263-1991
Overseas call (519) 396-9553 or Fax (519) 396-9554

About the
Author...

Ken
Vegotsky

...is a professional speaker, author and entrepreneur. Ken has given keynote addresses and seminars in the U.S.A. and Canada. He has been featured in print, radio and TV in the U.S.A., Canada, Australia, New Zealand, United Kingdom and a host of other countries.

*"**Ken is the Victor Frankl of our day** ,"* noted Dottie Walters, President of Walters Speakers Bureau and author of *Speak & Grow Rich.*

Mark Victor Hansen, New York Times #1 bestselling co-author of *Chicken Soup for the Soul,* says Ken's work is, ***"Brilliant and Illuminating."***

"In recognition of being seen as a model of courage and hope for others, who demonstrates to all of us the nobility of the human spirit..." begins the Clarke Institute Psychiatric Foundation nomination of Ken for a *Courage To Come Back Award.* These awards were originated by the St. Francis Health Foundation of Pittsburgh, PA.

Ken has served on the boards of NACPAC (affiliate of the American Chronic Pain Association) and a half-way home for mentally challenged people in transition. After numerous inspirational speeches, Ken was encouraged by listeners to tell his story.

His National Bestseller, ***The Ultimate Power*** shares his captivating first-person account of his near-death experience, garnished with proven keys for unlocking your personal power.

Discover ***How to Make Love With Life***™ and you'll feel embraced by caring and compassion as you share his moving experience.